For ALAN & PAM.

Jeff

MENDOCINO ROOTS & RIDGES

WINE NOTES FROM AMERICA'S GREENEST WINE REGION

BY HEIDI CUSICK DICKERSON

PHOTOGRAPHY BY TOM LIDEN

MENDOCINO GRASSROOTS PUBLICATIONS

MENDOCINO COUNTY MUSEUM

MENDOCINO COUNTY, CALIFORNIA

Enjoy!

Heidi Cusick Dickerson

Tom Liden

Mendocino Roots & Ridges

Wine Notes From America's Greenest Wine Region

www.RootsAndRidges.com

Copyright 2012

Mendocino County Museum

Mendocino Grassroots Publications

400 East Commercial Street

Willits, California 95490

(707) 459-2736

www.mendocinomuseum.org/

Library of Congress Cataloging-in-Publication Control # 2012948218

ISBN 978-0-9748934-7-1

Book design and layout by Kiersten Hanna

Printed in Canada

AUTHOR AND PHOTOGRAPHER DEDICATION

This book is the culmination of the work of many in Mendocino County's winegrowing community. It began with a column called "Wine Notes" in the *Ukiah Daily Journal* that took Heidi into her neighbors' vineyards, tasting rooms, kitchens and cellars and grew into a vision with Tom's photographs capturing the vines, buds, vintners and the unique scenery of Mendocino County.

A barrel full of thanks goes to our editors:
Nancy McLelland
Ann Thornhill
Cynthia Frank, Cypress House
Alison Glassey, Mendocino County Museum
Alison de Grassi

PUBLISHER'S DEDICATION

The Mendocino County Museum, a regional museum of history and culture, is honored to publish this book, which describes in words and photos the unique character of the wines and the people of Mendocino County.

Sales of the book will benefit the Museum's Wine History Project, which gathers the heritage of winemaking in Mendocino County, through recording and preserving oral histories, collecting wine equipment, artifacts, archives and photos, and creating exhibits and educational programs on Mendocino County viticulture.

This book is dedicated to the people who established the roots of winemaking in Mendocino County, and those who are nurturing that heritage today.

Special thanks go to Heidi Dickerson and Tom Liden for crafting words and images infused with their love for Mendocino wine culture. Thank you to Kiersten Hanna who skillfully brought all the elements together in a beautifully designed book and to Cynthia Frank of Cypress House, who was a steady, knowledgeable, and encouraging guide to the process of publishing.

CONTENTS

Foreword

Paul Dolan

As someone who has passionately farmed grapes using organic and biodynamic practices for nearly three decades in Mendocino County, I am inspired by this collection of stories about some of the winemakers who care as much about our environment as they do about their craft. I have had the good fortune to practice my beliefs about how to be successful while still being sustainable as it applies to the land, the company and my co-workers.

Being part of Mendocino County for so long, first with Fetzer Vineyards for twenty-seven years and as a former partner in the Mendocino Wine Company, has provided platforms from which to showcase new sustainable business practices that reach out beyond the next four quarters, beyond the next five years to consider what's ahead for the next generation. I first put down these words when I wrote "True to Our Roots: Fermenting a Business Revolution" in 2003.

Never were they truer than now. As you will see from Tom Liden's photographs of the outstanding natural beauty in Mendocino, the incentive to preserve and protect our resources is around us every day. The biggest struggles in our region have been about the best way to go forward. We are learning that there is a new model in which growth is not always the most important economic indicator.

Most of the wineries in Mendocino County are small, family-owned. A shared sense of values to produce a great product at a fair price keeps us going. Heidi's vignettes of seventy-plus proprietors and winemakers

give a glimpse into how we do business in Mendocino County. Tom's photos capture the magnificent natural resources, vineyards and evocative details.

I invite you to take a closer look and use this book to whet your appetite and join us at a tasting room, a farmers' market, on a wild mushroom forage, a fishing boat charter or at one of the excellent dining establishments on the coast and inland Mendocino County.

MENDOCINO COUNTY AGRICULTURAL CROP REPORT, 2010

Mendocino County leads California in organic wine acreage with nearly four thousand acres in ten distinct appellations. In addition to wine grapes, Mendocino produces over three thousand acres of organic fruits, nuts, and vegetable and forage crops. The commitment to sustainable agriculture takes many forms, including thousands of acres that are farmed biodynamically or under conservation programs such as Fish Friendly Farming. This commitment to sustainable farming enjoys strong community support with ten certified farmers markets and numerous Community Supported Agriculture farms [where consumers subscribe to produce, meat and cheese deliveries]. This approach to sustainability extends to silvaculture, with Mendocino County modeling sustainable forestry by managing forests not only for timber production, but also for watershed health, biodiversity, fisheries and wildlife. With the coastal zone and numerous inland valleys, Mendocino supports a wide diversity of agricultural crops, making Mendocino County the agricultural gem of the north coast.

INTRODUCTION

This place we call Mendocino has nurtured inhabitants with its benevolent climate, great soil and wild edibles from land and sea. The original population of Pomo Indians feasted on mussels, abalone, crab, salmon and rockfish. They hunted game and gathered berries, greens, mushrooms and acorns. More than ten tribes live in Mendocino County and tribal celebrations still center around food, including tributes to the acorn, surf fish and abalone.

Mendocino viticulture began in the 1850s. Thwarted gold miners found fertile valleys to grow profitable crops and hillsides to plant wine grapes. In the beginning, Italian settlers grew grapes for their homemade wine, but by the turn of the twentieth century, some three thousand acres of winegrapes were under cultivation.

In 1997, when I wrote *Mendocino: The Ultimate Wine and Food Lover's Guide*, there were thirty-six wineries. Today there are more than ninety, and nearly a quarter of all the grapes grown here are organic, more than any other winegrowing region can claim. Frey Vineyards in Redwood Valley is the world's first all-organic winery and is now Demeter Certified Biodynamic®. Fetzer Vineyards, under the leadership of Paul Dolan, switched to organic

grape growing in the 1980s and continues to gain recognition for sustainable business and winery practices. Bonterra Vineyards is also Demeter Certified Biodynamic®. Parducci, Mendocino's oldest continuously operating winery, is the world's first carbon neutral winery.

In Hopland, Real Goods, which sold the first home solar panel in the country, and the Solar Living Institute attract thousands of people every year to learn about energy, water, wind and other ecological home improvements. With more than two dozen solar companies in the county, it is not surprising to find solar-powered winery equipment, lights, pumps and soon, even tractors. Biodiesel increasingly powers trucks and farm equipment and is a growing industry fueled by companies like Yokayo Biofuels in Ukiah.

Mendocino's diverse and sparsely populated geography helped make our county home to the back-to-the-land movement of the 1970s. Their organic farming and buying local values have continued into the present generation. In 2004, Mendocino County was the first to ban the cultivation of genetically modified plants (GMOs). Ukiah Brewing Company is America's first all-organic brewpub. Farmers' markets in Mendocino, Ukiah,

Willits, Fort Bragg, Boonville and Laytonville showcase the local bounty from fruits and vegetables to meat, poultry and eggs.

Mediterranean influences imported by the early immigrants continue with the growing of olives, sunflowers and lavender, and the making of artisanal goat and cow cheese at small farms.

Most of Mendocino's wineries and vineyards are still family-owned. Vintners like Charlie Barra, John Parducci, Ted Bennett, Deborah Cahn, Milla Handley, Greg Graziano, Paul Dolan and the Fetzer, Frey, Nelson, Venturi, Bartolomei, Zeni and Brutocao families pride themselves on their Mendocino heritage and family proprietorships.

Mendocino's agricultural heritage is concentrated along the Russian River and the Navarro River watersheds. Glenn McGourty's chapter on *Dirt, Climate and Geography* explains the special terroir that is Mendocino County.

The profiles in this book are grouped by various characteristics that distinguish the wineries in Mendocino County. In these vignettes, you will meet some of the winemakers and grape growers whose history, heritage and philosophies make Mendocino unique in the wine world. Mendocino vintners include an eclectic mix of old-timers, back-to-the-landers, entrepreneurs and mavericks. Their stories are interspersed among Tom Liden's stunning photographs.

A section on resources includes visitor information, descriptions of wine clubs, and a seasonal sampling of annual festivals and wine events around the county.

The last chapter on Wine Routes gives an overview of some of the highlights found on the three major touring areas in Mendocino County. The routes are along Highway 101 from Hopland to Laytonville, Highway 128 from Yorkville through Anderson Valley to the coast, and Highway 1 along the Mendocino Coast.

Nearly a hundred wineries are found in Mendocino County. Their names, websites and phone numbers are included with the Wine Route where they or their tasting room are found. Some wineries in Mendocino County do not have tasting rooms open to the public. Please check each winery's website to determine its current location and hours before visiting.

The Mendocino County Museum, home of the Mendocino Wine History Project, and Mendocino's wine community have generously supported this book. Tom's photos evoke the wild and historic beauty of the roots, ridges, vineyards, hills, valleys, coastline, small towns and winding roads where vintners have chosen to make some of the best wine in the world. We invite you to join us to taste, discover and learn more about this green, cool and familial place we call home—Mendocino.

DIRT, CLIMATE, GEOGRAPHY

MENDOCINO COUNTY HAS IT ALL

GLENN MCCOURTY

Mendocino County, at latitude 39 degrees north (about the same latitude as both the tip of Southern Italy and Washington, DC) incorporates 3,878 square miles, larger than Delaware (2,489 square miles). Sparsely populated with about 89,000 people, the terrain ranges from sea level to nearly 7,000 feet.

Seventy percent of the county is covered with forests including redwood, Douglas fir, mixed evergreen and deciduous oak trees. North America's tallest oak tree, some of the world's largest redwoods, and America's biggest chestnut tree are in Mendocino County. Ninety-nine percent of the vineyards are located in the Upper Russian River and the Navarro River watersheds.

Geology and Soils: Seven million years ago the land known as Mendocino County emerged from the ocean, formed by underwater mountains that were constantly moved by earthquakes. Over millions of years, a huge east–west collision between the Pacific and North American tectonic plates uplifted the Coast Range Mountains that border the Pacific Ocean. Marine sediment soils mixed with grey-green serpentine in the earth's crust beneath the ocean floor formed molten material that uplifted and cooled.

The tectonic force known as the San Andreas Fault moves in a north–south direction, its path moving offshore under the ocean near Point Arena. The San Andreas meets the Mendocino Fault and the Cascadian subduction zone at a tectonic point known by geologists as the Mendocino Triple Junction, a very seismically active area.

In short, Mendocino is a mountainous region that is geologically unstable with little flat ground. The Coast Range straddling the west side of Mendocino County contains more serpentine-based rocks, whereas the Mayacamas Mountains on the east side are mixed with sandstone and volcanic rocks.

The best agricultural soils are formed from weathered sandstones and volcanic stone. These soils tend to be buff to reddish in color and found in upland areas. Mendocino's early grape growers were drawn to the red benchlands where they planted Zinfandel, Carignane and Petite Sirah. The soils on these hillsides are the oldest, shallowest and least fertile, making them at the time less expensive.

Redwood Valley, known for the red dirt, became identified as "Little Italy" because of the Italians who came at the turn of the century. They found that the red soil has moderate amounts of clay, good for holding moisture if you are dry land farming, while the frost that could decimate bottomland crops tended to roll down the hills.

Down slope on the valley bottoms the soils become younger, a bit sandier, deeper and more fertile. Almost all were formed as alluvial materials transported by rivers and streams. The early settlers planted hops, pears and prunes, along with grains and vegetables. Later they turned to grapes. Chardonnay and Sauvignon Blanc grow well in the bottom land soils along the Russian River valley where the soils are dark brown or blackish due to the abundant organic material they contain.

Because of the mixed geology and mountainous nature of the county, there are places where the soil literally changes every one hundred feet, making it necessary to plant many small blocks to match with variety, rootstocks and irrigation schedules.

Climate: Mendocino County has a classic Mediterranean climate characterized by cool, wet winters and warm, dry summers. With mountainous terrain and proximity to the coast, Mendocino is home to numerous microclimates. The cold Pacific Ocean is a dominant climatic force, resulting in average temperatures below seventy degrees most of the year. Foggy nights, cool mornings and diurnal winds are typical throughout the county.

The weather becomes warmer the farther away you get from the coast. Anderson Valley has considerable marine influence up the Navarro River. Its practical limit for grapegrowing is the "Deep End," a Boontling term (see Putting Anderson Valley on the Map) for the hamlet of Navarro. Varietals that ripen in cool areas such as Pinot Noir, Chardonnay, Gewurztraminer and Riesling grow here. Heading southeast along Highway 128 toward Boonville, the weather becomes warm enough for Sauvignon Blanc and Merlot.

Yorkville Highlands, located southeast and up ridge on Highway 128 is the headwaters of both the Navarro River and Dry Creek (Sonoma County) and the name of one of Mendocino's American Viticulture Areas (AVA) or appellations. Saddle winds blow through the hills in the afternoon making the area cool enough to grow quality Pinot Noir, but warm enough to ripen Merlot, Syrah and even Cabernet Sauvignon. Most of the vineyards are planted to red varieties, although Sauvignon Blanc from Yorkville is excellent.

Inland Mendocino County along the Highway 101 corridor experiences a pronounced drop in temperature at night due to the proximity of the cool Pacific Ocean air and intensity of "zephyrs," diurnal breezes that pick up when the rising valley heat meets the cool evening air. It is not uncommon in the summer for the temperature difference between the coast and inland to vary as much as fifty degrees. This swing helps the fruit to ripen while retaining acidity, thus retaining bright fruit-forward flavors and allowing the wines to age well.

The southernmost area in the Russian River watershed around Hopland is at the lowest elevation and has a slightly longer growing season. Cabernet Sauvignon grows especially well in upland vineyards around this part of the county. Moving north, the Ukiah Valley is a little higher and wider and most of Mendocino's grape varietals grow here.

The uphill benches near Talmage, east of Ukiah, and Calpella in Redwood Valley are suited for red grape production and home to head-pruned heritage Zinfandel, Petite Sirah and Carignane vines.

The growing season in Mendocino County occurs almost two weeks later than Napa and Sonoma Counties. Wine grapes that ripen at a cooler, later time of the year produce bright fruit flavors, good acidity and a long bottle life. Wines like Pinot Noir, Gewurztraminer, Riesling, Zinfandel and Cabernet Sauvignon exhibit intense flavor profiles because of the unique weather found in Mendocino County. The downside is that some years the weather can be very challenging to ripen fruit if the year is extremely cool and fall rains come too early.

Most seasons, Mendocino County grows flavorful, high quality fruit. The numerous microclimates formed by changes in slope, direction and proximity to the ocean provide many treasured spots for growing wine grapes and wine. From the tiny front yard plot of vines to those who own hundreds of acres, such as the historic Pauli family from Redwood Valley and the renowned Napa Valley maestro Andy Beckstoffer, Mendocino's diversity appeals to growers with many interests and passions.

So Italian...

The Mendocino wine story begins in the 1850s when Italian immigrants joined those disillusioned with the California Gold Rush and headed further westward. Lured by landscape and climate similar to their homeland, they settled on benchlands and in fertile valleys along the Russian and Navarro Rivers. From the 1890s until the early 1900s, another wave of Italians immigrated to Mendocino County, settling in Redwood and Ukiah Valleys, and the mountains above Yorkville on Fish Rock Road where many worked in the tan oak bark industry. In 1896, Giovanni and Sylvia Zarucchi planted a field blend of Zinfandel, Barbera and Carignane vines that continue to produce on what is now the Zeni Ranch near Yorkville. The wineries featured in this section are representative of the Italian influences you'll find in Mendocino. Other Italian names are found throughout this book. Two of the oldest families, Parducci and Milone, are in other sections. On wine lists around the country, you'll find references to Mendocino vineyards belonging to grape-growing families with names like Ciapusci, Zaina, Bartolomei, Pacini, Pallini, Venturi, Ricetti, Giannecchini, Testa and Milovina. They carry on the Old World traditions and some tend the same grapes planted by their great-grandparents. A tour of Mendocino's family-owned wineries and vineyards offers a step back in time and also a leap into the future where farmers are using renewable energy as well as organic farming techniques like their ancestors.

BARRA OF MENDOCINO
DEAN OF MENDOCINO VINO

NONNO GIUSEPPE WINES
AN ITALIAN-AMERICAN STORY

BRUTOCAO
ITALIAN STYLE IN HOPLAND

GRAZIANO
LOCAL LEGEND

CHIARITO
FATTA A MANO

TESTA RANCH
NEGRO Y BIANCO

JOHN PARDUCCI - "MR. MENDOCINO"

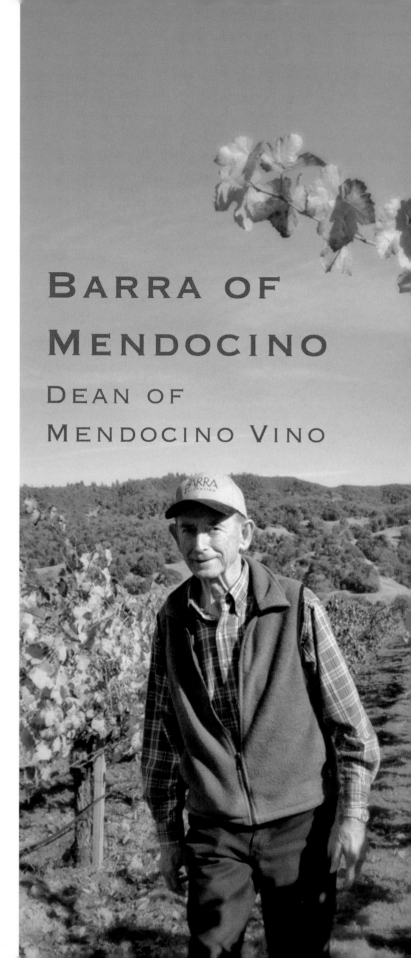

In the early 1900s Charlie Barra's grandparents immigrated to Mendocino County from the Piedmont region in Italy, where both had worked in vineyards.

In 1945, while still in high school, Charlie leased a vineyard. When it came time for harvest, he went to his principal to say he needed to cut back or quit school.

"He wasn't happy with that," says Charlie, "because I was class president and he wanted me to go to college. But I convinced him to let me go to school half day so I could farm the rest of the time." Charlie went to school in the morning and farmed in the afternoons and evenings, sometimes working until midnight. After his first harvest, Charlie's income was three times that of his principal.

"I told the principal how much I was getting for my grapes, and he agreed that we made a good decision," says Charlie with glee. The next year, however, the bottom fell out of the grape market and with his income. "I got a lesson in farming," says Charlie.

Since that 1945 harvest, Charlie Barra has been growing and promoting Mendocino grapes. In the 1930s and 1940s most of California's wine grapes were produced for bulk red and white wines. In the 1950s, ahead of his time, Charlie planted varietals including Pinot Noir, Pinot Blanc, Riesling, Cabernet Sauvignon and Chardonnay.

BARRA OF MENDOCINO
DEAN OF MENDOCINO VINO

A leader in forming the California North Coast Grape Growers' Association, which established the first wine-growing appellation—North Coast—in the United States, Charlie mentored several generations of Mendocino winegrowers and led the planting of varietal grapes on the North Coast.

For fifty years, he sold grapes from his Redwood Valley ranch to wineries in Napa, Sonoma, Livermore and Mendocino. "You know what a lot of famous wineries to the south of us have in common?" he asks, "Mendocino grapes!"

Always looking for a way to expand the visibility of Mendocino wines, Charlie and his wife Martha purchased the old Weibel winery and tasting room in 1995. Their showplace event facility on Highway 101 in Redwood Valley was originally built in the 1970s and modeled to look like an inverted champagne glass to honor Weibel's signature bubbly.

Inside the circular brick building and looking up gracefully curved beams feels like being beneath a giant gilled mushroom. The reference is appropriate given Charlie's mushroom hunting prowess, an Italian pastime handed down by his parents. Soon after the first rains Charlie disappears into the woods to gather porcini (*Boletus edulis*) for dinner and drying.

In the 1990s, Charlie and Martha launched their Barra of Mendocino wine. "It was a practical move," he says. "In addition to having more control over the harvest time of your grapes, making wine improves your options by going from perishable grapes to age-able wine. Besides," Charlie points out, "in Italy grape growers crush all their own grapes, even though much of it goes to bulk wine."

The Barras' vineyards now include 175 acres, certified organic since 1988. Charlie loves to point out that "we didn't call our growing organic for the first twenty five years!" Fifty acres of organic Zinfandel and Cabernet surround the tasting room. In 2007 Charlie and Martha planted nearly 200 olive trees at another vineyard, just east of Ukiah near Lake Mendocino.

"A guy who is eighty one years old and planting trees for olive oil has to be a compulsive farmer or else has something wrong with him," laughs Charlie, known for relating his experiences going on seven decades. His commitment to his heritage and organic farming bring continued praise from many local grape growers who credit Charlie as their mentor. In 2011 he was honored by Slow Food at a special dinner where he was commended by Slow Food's founder Carlo Petrini.

The Barras grow all the grapes for their Barra of Mendocino label, which includes Zinfandel, Petite Sirah, Pinot Noir, Cabernet Sauvignon, Sangiovese, Chardonnay, Pinot Blanc, and Charlie's favorite, the luscious fragrant and sweet Muscat Canelli. In 2003 they began bottling wine under the Girasole (Italian for sunflower) label to promote their organic Cabernet, Sangiovese,

Pinot Noir, Zinfandel, Pinot Blanc, Chardonnay, Merlot and "Hybrid Red."

Barra's historic tasting room is a great venue for weddings and other indoor and outdoor events. Barra events are especially noteworthy. Martha is a renowned Mendocino County hostess and their winery events such as the annual Mendocino Wine & Mushroom Fest dinner in November are feasts to remember.

NONNO GIUSEPPE

AN ITALIAN-AMERICAN STORY

Nonno Giuseppe Zinfandel has a label with old-world appeal. Straightforward die-cut with a simple gold border, it features the photograph of Nonno Giuseppe, a grandfather whose story is the everyman tale of Italian families that immigrated to the United States in search of a better life in the early twentieth century.

When the decision was made to put the historic family photo of Nonno Giuseppe Rovera on their wine, Rovera's granddaughter, Lucille Neese, and her husband William Marion (Bill) Neese and their son Bill Neese created an icon. The wine is made from grapes their family has grown on their ranch in Redwood Valley for more than 100 years. "Our family has been in the wine and grape business practically since my grandfather came to Calpella in 1906," says Lucille.

Giuseppe was born in 1868 in the Piedmont region of Italy. In 1903, he immigrated to the United States, eventually landing in California and sending for his wife Lucia. She traveled with two-year-old Maria and three-month-old Charlie (Lucille's father) to Ellis Island and then across the country to join Giuseppe in California. "Can you imagine speaking no English and traveling with an infant all the way across the country? What a brave thing," says Lucille. "It's a typical Italian story."

In 1906 the Roveras settled in the Redwood Valley area because the geography reminded them of home. Giueseppi planted grapes and sold them for his livelihood. He and Lucia had one more son, Pete. All three children, even after they married, continued working in the vineyards, as did their spouses and the grandkids. In addition to Lucille, another of Giuseppe's grandchildren is Mendocino County's "dean of Mendocino winegrowing," Charlie Barra.

In 1946, at age 14, Lucille met Bill Sr. soon after he and his family moved to Redwood Valley. "We went together for four years before getting married in 1950," says Lucille. Bill and Lucille purchased 18 acres across the street from Lucille's family vineyard on the corner of West and School Roads in Redwood Valley. Now both properties are part of Neese Vineyards.

For years Bill worked as a logger and had a fleet of trucks. In the 1970s, he purchased the old Lindberg's Hardware store in Calpella. His son Bill, who went to UC Davis and studied viticulture, became a partner in the vineyard and winery. Daughter Susie Mathis lives with her husband Greg and three children in Calpella.

Through the decades, the Neeses worked other jobs and farmed sixty eight acres of vineyards. "In the old days, like everyone else, we sold our grapes to Italian Swiss Colony in Asti in Sonoma County," says Bill Sr.

In 1999 the Neeses decided to make their own wine. The first vintage, the 1999 Nonno Giuseppe Zinfandel won Best of Show at the San Francisco Chronicle competition. The 2000 Nonno Giuseppe Zinfandel was declared the state's best Zinfandel at the 2002 California State Fair.

They have since added Chardonnay, Cabernet Sauvignon and Merlot with Nonno Giuseppe on the label. Their tasting room on the corner of West and School Roads draws the crowds on festival weekends such as the Taste of Redwood Valley in June. Lucille, a great cook, is known for her gnocchi. And her spaghetti sauce is legendary!

BRUTOCAO CELLARS

ITALIAN STYLE IN HOPLAND

From the Venetian-style lion celebrating St. Mark's Square on their wine label to their tasting room, restaurant and bocce courts, the Brutocao family brings the best of their Italian heritage to their wines and tasting rooms in Hopland and Anderson Valley.

The father of the late patriarch Len Brutocao was from Treviso near Venice. Len's wife Marty is part of the Bliss family, longtime grape growers in Sonoma County. In 1943 Marty's father, Irv Bliss, bought property east of Hopland where he had sheep, prunes and grapes. In 1974 the family planted 200 acres of grapes including a block of Zinfandel, now considered old vine.

For several decades Len and his sons were in highway construction in southern California. In

1994, the Brutocaos wanted a change and a year later moved to Hopland, where they started the winery and purchased the old Hopland High School building for their tasting room. Brothers Steve, David and Lenny do the operations and manage the business.

Inside the Hopland tasting room, a hand-painted fresco features St. Mark's Square. Tiled floors and marble tabletops, arched alcoves and a selection of glassware, kitchenware and linens evoke Italianate style.

More than two dozen wines are open for tasting each day. In addition to classic varietals such as Cabernet and Chardonnay, Brutocao is gaining recognition for Italian varietals: Barbera, Primitivo, Dolcetto and Sangiovese and their award-winning blend of the four known as Quadriga.

In the summer local bocce teams compete, drink wine and eat crispy pizzas from a wood-fired oven. On balmy evenings the sun sets against the western hills backlighting the terraces of lavender, roses and olive trees. In 2002 the Brutocaos opened a second tasting room on Highway 128 in Anderson Valley. Appropriate to the location, the roomy rustic tasting room has a Mendocino-style redwood exterior and unmistakable Italian hospitality inside.

GRAZIANO FAMILY OF WINES
LOCAL LEGEND

Greg Graziano is known throughout the wine industry for his wine talents, his work ethic and for his Italian heritage. His grandparents came to Mendocino County in 1918 from the Piedmont region of Italy.

Greg's grandfather Vincenzo and great-uncle Hugo Graziano grew their first grapes in Redwood Valley during Prohibition. They shipped the grape juice to the East Coast for altar wine. Greg's dad, Joseph, met and married Greg's mom, Monti Lee, when he was in the military. They settled on the family ranch, where Greg and his brother Mark were raised. Then, in 1970, on what should have been a normal day in the vineyards, Joseph Graziano was accidentally and tragically electrocuted at the age of thirty-nine, when Greg was sixteen.

Greg went on to study viticulture at the University of California at Davis but his main education came from the many wineries he has

been associated with over the last thirty years. Known by his friends in the industry for never meeting a grape he didn't like, Greg has made wine for more than twenty brands.

In 1976, he helped another longtime Mendocino winemaker Jim Milone start Milano Winery. Greg was also involved with other Mendocino wineries including Olson, Tysseling, Baccala, Scharffenberger, La Crema and Hidden Cellars.

In 1988, between sourcing grapes and making wine for others Greg found time to create the first of his four brands, Domaine Saint Gregory.

These days, Graziano concentrates on his own wines. He is involved in every aspect of his wine business, from the color and design of the labels to the names of the brands and the wines in the bottles.

Domaine Saint Gregory is his Burgundian brand. The wines include Pinot Noir, Pinot Meunier and Chardonnay as well as Pinotage, a South African hybrid.

In 1991, while making wine in a converted hop kiln at Lowell Stone's Fox Hill vineyard on Old River Road, Greg was inspired by Stone's sixty acres of Italian varietals, and created the Monte Volpe label. Monte Volpe, which is Italian for fox hill, features the classic grapes of Tuscany such as Tocai Friulano, Pinot Grigio, Sangiovese, Montepulciano and Peppolino. The label displays assorted images of a fox and it's entertaining to see how many foxes you can count on it. Here's a hint for one—the shape of the label is a fox head.

His second Italian wine label is Fattoria Enotria, which features the grapes of the Piedmont region of Italy. Varietals include white Arneis and Cortese, a slightly sweet Moscato, and red Barbera, Dolcetto and Nebbiolo.

Greg put his own name on his latest brand, Graziano, which is mainly vineyard-designated Zinfandel, but also includes Chenin Blanc, Sauvignon Blanc, Petite Sirah and Zinfandel Rosé.

The grapes for Greg Graziano's wines come from a dozen or more vineyards around Mendocino County, many having an Italian heritage. "I love the family traditions of the old growers and I find their grape prices to be fair, which allows me to price my wine fairly," says Graziano. His wife Trudi is the winery's compliance guru. She and Greg have two daughters, Isabella and Alexandra.

In addition to sourcing fruit from around Mendocino, the Grazianos have a twenty-acre vineyard in Potter Valley that they named Nube Bianco for the big white cumulus clouds that form over the eastern hills in the summer. "Having my own vineyard, olive trees and a huge garden with my family make this the most fulfilling time of my life," he says. He just planted three hundred olive trees and a few more varieties of white wine grapes—all Italian.

CHIARITO

John Chiarito could have been born a hundred years ago in Italy. One look at his vineyard, Italian-style farmhouse, pergola, olive and walnut trees, and the outdoor brick oven and it's obvious that John Chiarito (pronounced kee-a-ree' toe) cares deeply about the best of the old Italian ways.

"My family came to this country from southern Italy. When I was a kid, we would spend every Sunday with my grandparents, aunts, uncles and cousins, eating great food and drinking homemade wine," says John. "So when I bought my land on the Talmage bench and decided to build my own home and create my own winery, I made it a tribute to my grandparents and their way of life."

He kept a border of walnut trees from the old orchard on the five-acre property he purchased in 1988. In 1989 he dug the foundation for the charming craftsman house that could be a contemporary Italian dwelling somewhere outside Naples, where it so happens his grandparents on his mother's side were born.

John built a brick oven for cooking pizza and roasting whole pigs. A garden next to the vineyard sprouts squash, fennel, sunflowers, artichokes, basil, oregano and tomatoes. A traditional vine-covered pergola shades the outdoor eating area. A few steps away is the wine cellar, where wine is aged in barrels and haunches of hanging prosciutto cure from the rafters.

Fatto a mano is Chiarito's motto, and the distinctive reddish orange and green label pays homage to the Italian flag. In the background is the watermark of his father Americo's hand, which was drawn by John's brother. The original lithograph hangs

FATTO A MANO

over his fireplace. "Everything here is touched by hand—*fatto a mano*," he explains, "the vineyard, the wine, garden, olives, house and my bread."

John Chiarito makes wine from Zinfandel, Petite Sirah and a couple of Italian varietals—Negroamaro and Nero d'Avola. He was the first to get permission to use Negroamaro and Nero d'Avola on a wine label in the United States. At a tasting of the Talmage Tasters, a thirty-plus-year-old wine tasting group, Chiarito's Nero d'Avola beat out ten Italian versions of the varietal as the favorite. "I was stunned and very proud," he says.

From the beginning of the winery John's dad, Americo Chiarito, corked every bottle and worked every harvest until he passed away at 96 in 2011 shortly after the birth of John's son Gabriel. Treasuring the old, John has a collection of antique tools including an adze used for barrel making, pruning shears and a well-used old funnel. He pieced together plows from 1930s-era parts to till between the vines on his dry-farmed benchland.

With a commitment to honor the good things of life, John says, "I like to think I've created a little bit of southern Italy right here in Ukiah."

Chiarito has a wine club for lovers of the old Italian way of life. Members are invited to a tasting of his wood-fired pizza when picking up their wine, special Italian home-cooking lessons with lunch, and a popular pig-roast party in the summer. Everything done by hand.

TESTA RANCH

NEGRO Y BIANCO

"We're doing this to preserve our family heritage," says Maria Testa Martinson, great-granddaughter of Gaetano and Maria Testa who established Testa Vineyards in 1912. A lovingly restored farmhouse and the release of Testa Vineyards wines honor five generations of Testas in Calpella as the next generation segues into the future, Italian birthright firmly in place.

The Testa brand, Simply Black and White Wines, copies the old style of wine that blended a variety of red grapes or white grapes.

Gaetano Testa, a native of Gallarate, Italy, arrived with two brothers in San Francisco in 1906. "It was the same day as the earthquake," says his ninety-five-year-old daughter Rose Marie Testa Indelicato. Rose, her sister-in-law Lee Testa and neighbor Guido

Venturi are "treasures from our eldest generation," says Maria.

Gaetano quickly found work clearing the rubble and helping to rebuild San Francisco. After three years in the city, Gaetano and his brothers took a train north. As the train chugged through Ukiah to the Calpella station Gaetano was struck by the similarities of the surrounding countryside to his homeland. His brothers returned to the city. But Gaetano stayed and sent to Italy for his wife Maria and their son Victor.

"They cleared the land with Belgian horses and dynamite," says Maria. "Whenever Nonno (Gaetano) got money he bought land." Nonna (Maria) worked hard helping to burn the slash. She also made bread to sell, cooked and took care of the children. In 1927 they built the family farmhouse on a knoll surrounded by vineyards.

Maria's great-grandfather on her mother's side was Battista Garzini. His Battista Winery, which operated from 1910 to 1936, may have been the first bonded winery in Mendocino County. The stone remnants are still visible on the east side of Lake Mendocino.

The Testas made wine in the farmhouse cellar, where many a party was held during Prohibition. Some of the old winemaking equipment like the grape-stained crusher and the redwood fermentation tank are being put back into use.

The ranch is now twenty-five acres, having been reduced when Highway 101 was routed through Gaetano's property, and later when he sold acreage to the nearby mill. The family vineyards include Carignane, Petite Sirah, Zinfandel, Grenache, Charbono and Barbera.

As the winemaker for Testa wines, "I am surrounded in my family by winemaking history," says Maria, the mother of four children. Maria credits her family and friends with the Testa–Martinson's symbiotic transition from a grape-growing family to their new winemaking and innkeeping status. The refurbished family farmhouse is now a vacation rental. The barn is an event site and the tasting room is in one of the historic sheds. Maria's husband Rusty did all the remodeling and improvements.

"Having this vacation rental is an invitation to people from the city to come and find out what it's like to experience a real working place in this beautiful valley," she says. "There is so much here," adds Maria, "the vineyards, the pond for fishing, the proximity to Lake Mendocino, and only an hour to the redwoods and the coast."

The tasting room in the converted chicken coop is a tasteful barnwood-paneled room that opens to pond-side sitting and sipping.

Testa's Simply Black and White Wines are blends "just like my Nonno made from the grapes he grew," says Maria. "I make Testa wine to be fruity and not overbearing so it tastes good with everything—food, friends and family."

Green, Gold and Cow Horns

Mendocino County is known as America's greenest wine region because more grapes are grown organically here than in any other winegrowing area. Forty percent of California's organic crops are grown in Mendocino. In addition to having a high percentage of California Certified Organic Farms (CCOF), nearly a quarter of those grapes are also Demeter Certified Biodynamic®. To be a certified biodynamic sustainable entity, everything on the farm from the soil to the people, the climate to the geography, the animals to the plants is interrelated and needs to be considered. Equally important, 5,600 acres out of approximately 16,400 vineyard acres are certified Fish Friendly, which assures growing practices that protect Coho salmon and steelhead trout. Many more vineyards and farms use no pesticides or herbicides, but don't go through the laborious and expensive CCOF certification process. Some farmers in Mendocino created their own "Renegade" certification, a cost effective process that includes a precautionary principle requiring consideration of potential harm to animals and the environment. The wineries in this section are among the leaders in organic and biodynamic farming. Others in this book are: Masut, McFadden; Terra Sávia; Patianna, Jeriko Saracina; Yorkville; Handley; Barra; and Fetzer.

PARDUCCI WINE CELLARS
HISTORIC AND CARBON NEUTRAL

PAUL DOLAN
BIODYNAMIC VISIONARY

BONTERRA
A LESSON IN BIODYNAMIC

FREY
FAMILY AND FARM IN HARMONY

GOLDEN VINEYARD
FOR THE FAMILY

LE VIN
TALENTED DUO SHARE
ORGANIC FARM

Parducci Wine Cellars

Historic and Carbon Neutral

IN 2007, AND AGAIN IN 2009, PARDUCCI CELLARS RECEIVED CALIFORNIA'S HIGHEST ENVIRONMENTAL AWARD, THE GOVERNOR'S ENVIRONMENTAL AND ECONOMIC LEADERSHIP AWARD, RECOGNIZING IT AS THE NATION'S FIRST CARBON NEUTRAL WINERY AND FOR THEIR CONTINUING DEDICATION TO SOCIAL RESPONSIBILITY AND ENVIRONMENTALLY SOUND WINE-GROWING AND BUSINESS PRACTICES.

Mendocino County's oldest winery is also its greenest. As the first carbon neutral winery in the United States, Parducci Wine Cellars combines a commitment to minimizing their impact on the environment with respect for their history. Parducci is a family venture with a highly respected winemaking team.

First the history. In 1921, the pragmatic Adolph Parducci, an Italian immigrant from Tuscany planted grapes during Prohibition on the old home ranch just north of Ukiah. Parducci's signature Petite Sirah vineyard continues to this day. In 1932, Adolph built a winery and when Prohibition ended a year later he was ready to go. He was joined by his four sons, including Mendocino's wine patriarch, John Parducci, now of McNab Ridge Winery.

Fast forward to 2004 when the Thornhill family formed a partnership to purchase the old winery and vineyards. All former Texans, the Thornhill family includes parents Tommy and Ann and sons Tom and Tim. The new arrivals to Mendocino County settled into one of Mendocino's renowned vineyards,

La Ribera, on Old River Road south of Ukiah. "The idea was to create a place for our extended family," says Tim. "We were drawn by the potential of the wine industry in Mendocino County."

After purchasing La Ribera, the brothers were joined by their mom and dad, a retired investment and securities management executive. The senior Thornhills relocated from Houston to reside in La Ribera Ranch's Victorian cottage and assist with the 150-acre vineyard.

Two years later, Parducci winery was for sale. "We had vineyards and we saw purchasing Parducci as a business opportunity to create vertical integration from our grapes to making wine," says Tom. "It was a good fit," adds Tim.

The Thornhills formed the Mendocino Wine Company and purchased Parducci, a fully operating winery that included one of Mendocino County's most respected winemakers, Bob Swain. The next generation has also joined the Thornhills' Parducci team. Tim's daughter Kate Thornhill Beaman works the export market. Her husband Mark Beaman is the associate winemaker (look for him promoting "Wines that Rock"). And Tim's son, Chase Thornhill, is Parducci's marketing specialist.

Vestiges remain of the old winery, such as the popular mission-style tasting room with archways and Italian ceramic tiles. Inside the once state-of-the-art winery, built in the 1930s, seventeen- to twenty-thousand gallon vertical grain virgin redwood wine tanks fill one room and are still used for red wines.

The original Parducci cellar exhibits the reverence for things past. Old photos depict a bygone era of winemaking. An open ledger from the 1940s reveals grape purchases from vineyard owners whose relatives continue to sell their grapes to Parducci two generations later. A visit and tour of Parducci includes a lesson in what it takes to reduce your carbon footprint. The state-of-the-art wetlands demonstrate water recycling and are an aesthetic destination for myriad waterfowl and other wildlife. Solar panels bring power to the certified organic facility. In addition to being certified organic, Parducci also uses biodynamic preparations to spread among the vines at prescribed intervals to enrich the soil and vitalize the vines. Parducci published *The Green Winegrowing Handbook* that contains information on biodynamic, organic and sustainable practices.

Expanding the Parducci commitment to quality and value, the Thornhill family draws on Parducci's heritage to reinvigorate the venerable brand. In addition to Parducci's renowned Petite Sirah, Sauvignon Blanc and Sustainable Red and White blends, "a selection of new small lot blends forms the foundation of our historic winery's portfolio," says Chase.

PAUL DOLAN

BIODYNAMIC VISIONARY

IN 2002, PAUL DOLAN PRODUCED THE FIRST BIODYNAMIC WINEGROWERS SYMPOSIUM AND INTRODUCED THE CODE OF SUSTAINABLE WINE GROWING TO MEMBERS OF THE WINE INSTITUTE. SINCE THEN HE HAS LED DOZENS OF BIODYNAMIC EDUCATION "CAMPS" INVOLVING HUNDREDS OF PEOPLE IN THE WINE COMMUNITY.

"Rooted" is the first word that comes to mind when describing Paul Dolan. A fourth-generation winemaker, Paul comes from a family that is part of California's wine history.

Paul Dolan's winemaking roots reach on his mother's side to Italy. Great-grandfather Pietro Carlo Rossi immigrated to California and by 1881 was instrumental in creating the Italian Swiss Colony in Asti, south of Cloverdale in Sonoma County. Italian Swiss Colony was originally an agricultural colony organized to provide jobs for immigrants from northern Italy.

When the Colony decided to make wine, Paul's great-grandfather took on the duties. "They won the first medal for California Zinfandel in 1906 at a Paris competition," says Paul. The Rossi family ran the winery from the 1880s until the 1940s. On his father's side, Paul's grandmother was from another old California winemaking family. Her father started Concannon winery in Livermore in 1883.

Paul studied business at the University of Santa Clara and had a stint in the military. The pull to the land and his winemaking heritage led him to a degree in enology from Fresno State University in the mid-1970s. When Mendocino County beckoned and Barney Fetzer hired him, Paul became the first non-family member winemaker at Fetzer Vineyards.

Paul soon discovered what a difference organically grown grapes made in flavor. He often describes the first time he compared the taste of organic grapes alongside the same varietal raised with pesticides.

"It changed my way of looking at not only flavor, but what went into growing that flavor," he says in his book *True to Our Roots*.

In 1988, Fetzer released its first red wine grown from organically grown grapes. "It was a hard sell at first," Paul remembers. He met regularly with growers to enroll them in organic growing methods. He taught them about controlling pests with beneficial insects and putting in riparian borders between blocks of vines to provide diverse habitat that is essential in farming without pesticides. He's proud that the Chardonnay he planted in the organic vineyard at Valley Oaks in Hopland survived the 1990s influx of phylloxera that ruined many other vineyards.

With Paul at the helm, Fetzer focused on Jim Fetzer's biodynamically farmed vineyard in McNab Valley. They created a brand to showcase the all-organic grapes and the McNab ranch became home to the all-organic, biodynamic Bonterra winery.

With his sons, Jason and Heath, Paul purchased Dark Horse Ranch on Old River Road south of Ukiah. They grow seventy acres of certified organic and Demeter Certified Biodynamic® Cabernet Sauvignon, Petite Sirah, Syrah, Zinfandel, Grenache and Mourvedre.

In keeping with the biodynamic philosophy on the 160-acre ranch, 70 acres are vineyard, 20 acres remain in pasture and the rest in woodlands. Animals include four quarterhorses, three Dexter

cows, Dorper sheep, a hodgepodge of goats, and forty chickens that live in a movable chicken house in order to make best use of their scratching and bug-eating skills between the vine rows.

In 2002, Paul Dolan produced the first Biodynamic Symposium that included winegrowers from California, France and Australia. He also introduced the Code of Sustainable Wine Growing to members of the Wine Institute, an influential industry trade association. During his years at Fetzer, Paul was named *Wine & Spirits* magazine Winemaker of the Year seven years in a row.

Dolan's business model is based on what he coined the three E's—economic viability, environmental sustainability and employee equity. His wines exemplify the quality of the grapes grown on the family's organic and biodyanamic Dark Horse Ranch, as well as from other organic vineyards in Mendocino County.

"My goal with my wine is to support small family farms in the community and produce a high-end wine from their grapes," says the leading voice in biodynamic winegrowing, adding, "I'm committed to passing on a legacy to my kids, my family and the community."

Bonterra

A Lesson in Biodynamic

The beautiful setting of the Bonterra home ranch, located in McNab Valley southwest of Ukiah, is appropriate for a wine whose name translates to "good earth." Bonterra wines are made from California Certified Organic Farmers (CCOF) and Demeter Certified Biodynamic® grapes. First released in 1992, Bonterra leads production of organic wines in the United States.

When Jim Fetzer purchased the McNab Ranch in 1993, he turned to the biodynamic way of farming. "Biodynamic used to be thought of as way out there,"

says Bonterra's winemaker Bob Blue. He is referring to skeptics who point to such practices as farming by the phases of the moon and composting with dung-filled cow horns. Blue attributes the sustainability trailblazing by Fetzer Vineyards, Bonterra's owner, as helping change that idea.

What is biodynamic? The principles of biodynamic farming are attributed to Rudolf Steiner, an Austrian philosopher and social thinker. In 1924, responding to farmers concerned about poor soil conditions related to the use of chemicals and fertilizers, Steiner prescribed eight preparations related to the field and composting. He also prescribed holistic treatments for pests and weeds that call for habitat diversity, beneficial insects and the use of a variety of farm friendly animals and plants to bring about balance on the farm.

"Translating the principles into practice means living and working within the natural system you find at the ranch," says Bob. "It means putting natural habitat breaks between the blocks of grapes so that beneficial insects move in and help keep away unwanted bugs. The more diversity you have, the more long-term stability."

At Bonterra, lavender borders, olive trees, a cooperative vegetable garden for the employees, cover crops, grazing sheep and chickens and composted grape pomace add biodiversity to the vineyards, thus challenging the monoculture of conventional vineyards. The diversity replaces pesticides and chemical fertilizers.

"We include the hand of nature over the top of the vineyard instead of spraying it away," says Bob. The soil is nurtured by adding compost, and planting a diversity of cover crops, which contribute nutrients and valuable organic matter.

Using awards and growth of sales as indicators, the verdict is in the bottle. Bonterra's 2006 Chardonnay, made from one hundred percent organic grapes, was chosen as the first recipient of the first Green Wine Sweepstakes at the Mendocino County Fair Wine Competition. Bonterra's growth (5,000 cases to 350,000 cases in twenty years) mirrors the rise in popularity of all-organic products. Bonterra wines can be found throughout the US, as well as in thirty-five countries.

Bonterra wines also include Sauvignon Blanc, Viognier, Riesling, Muscat, Rosé, Merlot, Cabernet Sauvignon, Syrah and Zinfandel. The majority of the grapes for these wines come from estate vineyards farmed at the Bonterra home ranch. The rest come from Mendocino and Lake County vineyards. Dave Koball manages 1,200 acres of organic vines, of which more than 250 acres are biodynamic, for Bonterra and Fetzer in Mendocino County, with the assistance of Chad Boardman.

In addition to the single varietals, Bonterra added two iconic wines, the McNab and the Butler, to showcase its two namesake biodynamic-farmed estates. The McNab is a Bordeaux-style blend and the Butler a Rhône-style blend. "These wines show classic form and elegance," says Bob, adding, "What you get from farming biodynamically is balance."

Bonterra is owned by Concha y Toro, a family-owned Chilean winery that has a commitment to organic and sustainable winemaking. The Bonterra website is an enticing way to learn more about the wines and vineyards complete with video tours.

FREY VINEYARDS
FAMILY AND FARM IN HARMONY

The Frey family lives by organic and biodynamic tenets at their ranch and winery in Redwood Valley. Four generations of Freys live on the ranch and work in the family business. This includes most of the twelve children of matriarch Beba and her late husband Paul Frey, along with spouses and dozens of grandchildren.

Frey is the largest and the first all-organic winery in the United States and is a leader in Demeter Certified Biodynamic® designation. All Frey wine labels carry the certified organic label. It was the first winery in the United States to be authorized to add the Biodynamic® certification to their label.

In 1961, Beba and her late husband purchased the former Mexican land grant known as Spring Hill Ranch, near the headwaters of the Russian River. This matriarch works alongside more than forty-five members of her extended and enterprising

offspring. Since 1980, the Frey Ranch has grown from ninety-one to one thousand acres.

In addition to the spacious redwood home known as the Big House, other family homes are discreetly clustered around the property to minimize roads and maximize water and other service connections. In 1965, the family planted grapes because they wanted a crop deemed too valuable to lose when there was pressure to build a dam at the end of Redwood Valley for a reservoir.

For the first fifteen years, grapes from the original forty-acre vineyard were primarily sold to other wineries. In the 1970s, while studying astrophysics at the University of California in Santa Cruz, oldest son Jonathan met the famed horticulturist Alan Chadwick. Later, Jonathan followed Chadwick to Covelo in eastern Mendocino County in order to study organic farming. When he returned to the family ranch in 1980, he established the Frey family winery.

The winery is housed in a hand-hewn redwood building, trimmed along the rooflines with icicle-shaped wood shingles carved by one of the Frey brothers. Stainless tanks are wrapped with insulation and barrels are stacked in the cellar under the second-story office. Solar panels next to the wine warehouse provide three-quarters of the winery's power.

Between the winery and Beba's Big House is a large courtyard, where redwood slab tables and benches double as the tasting room as well as for family and nonprofit events. A well-used adobe oven is designed in the style of a sister-in-law's native Bolivian hometown.

Around the ranch, family-tended vegetable gardens sprout in sunny spots near apple and pear trees and between wooded areas and rambling borders of blueberries and raspberries. Hooded mergansers, mallards and wood ducks, and a pair of cormorants are often spotted on a small pond. Wildlife corridors are interspersed between vineyards and human habitation.

"In order to be Demeter Certified Biodynamic®, you have to put aside at least ten percent of the farm for diversity, allowing wild as well as domestic animals to coexist on the land," says Katrina Frey, who is married to Jonathan, and oversees Frey's wine marketing.

All of the grapes at the Frey Ranch have received Biodynamic® certification. "Demeter USA developed the first biodynamic wine standards," Katrina says, "Now we hope to get them in place internationally." Frey produces up to twenty different wines each year. Fifteen percent of the wine is labeled with the Biodynamic® logo and the rest is California Certified Organically Farm (CCOF) grown and produced.

The major difference between biodynamic and other organic wines is that Biodynamic® wine standards guide winemakers to produce wines that are minimally manipulated. Katrina says, "It is a natural extension of what we do."

Frey Vineyards is open by appointment and during their many events, including A Taste of Redwood Valley in June.

GOLDEN VINEYARDS
FOR THE FAMILY

Julie and Joe Golden approach their biodynamic, organic and Fish Friendly vineyard ventures with gusto. Their home ranch, known as Heart Arrow, sprawls upward at the top of the keyhole north of Ukiah in western Redwood Valley. Their other vineyard, the Fairbairn Ranch, lies along Old River Road in Hopland.

Julie grew up in Ukiah. Her father's family first grew hops and then planted grapes on South State Street and also on Tindall Ranch Road across the river in Talmage. Her father, Richard Mattern, still grows Zinfandel, Petite Sirah and Chardonnay.

"I grew up looking out the kitchen window at vineyards," says Julie. As an adult, her work in the high tech world led to living in Germany, where she met her husband Joe Golden, a trailblazer in high technology startups in Europe, China and the United States.

After living in Europe for eight years, Julie says that when it was time to have kids they came back

to Mendocino to find property. "Growing up out of doors is intrinsic to what kids need," she says. In 1997, the Goldens purchased 1,200 acres of the Heart Arrow Ranch.

Geographic diversity on the ranch includes an earthquake fault, peaks and meadows and the railway bed for the old Redwood Valley to Willits section of train tracks. To the west is Eagle Peak, and twenty-three miles farther is the coast. Extolling the virtues of the ranch's 750 to 3000-foot elevation and southwestern exposure, Julie notes that when

Ukiah is fogged in, the ranch is often clear.

Joe's favorite wine is Cabernet Sauvignon. His dream was to plant it on a hillside and Heart Arrow Ranch has plenty of south and west facing slopes. "When we planted Cabernet grapes, everyone laughed because Napa Valley was the leader in Cabernet," says Julie. However, they feel their site is special with its red vine series soils. They knew these hillsides had less extreme temperature variations than either valley vineyards or even famous Cabernet Vineyards to the south of Mendocino County.

The Goldens planted twenty-six acres in Cabernet, five and a half acres in Petite Sirah, and four and a half acres in Zinfandel. At Fairbairn Ranch, they grow twenty-two acres of Syrah.

In fulfilling the Biodynamic® biodiversity component, the Goldens also raise sheep, pigs, cattle and chickens as well as olives, fruit trees and a vegetable garden. Adam Gaska and Paula Manalo, whose company, Mendocino Organics, supplies food for everyone on the ranch, tend the garden and the animals. In addition, Mendocino Organics supplies produce to sixty other families, a restaurant, and other local businesses that subscribe to their CSA (Community Supported Agriculture). "We supply the infrastructure and Adam and Paula supply the labor and business acumen to manage the non-vineyard related products," says Julie.

Ninety-five percent of Golden Vineyard grapes are sold to wineries such as Mendocino Farms, Patianna and Elizabeth Spencer. Golden Cellars is part of the Coro Mendocino consortium and produces a Coro Mendocino Zinfandel blend. In her spare time, Julie helps promote Coro Mendocino.

"All that we do with Golden Cellars and Golden Vineyards contributes to our overall goal of leaving this bit of earth in a healthier state, and that's my legacy to my family," says Julie, "We do it all for them."

LE VIN WINERY AND VINEYARDS
TALENTED DUO SHARE ORGANIC FARM

He's a singer–songwriter and classically trained musician. She's a graphic artist related to Gumby. Together, Eric Levin and Holly Harman make wine. And they are WWOOFers.

World Wide Opportunities on Organic Farms was founded in the 1970s in Britain. WWOOF attracts young people who want to work on the farm in exchange for room and board. At Le Vin, WWOOFers may find themselves picking olives, helping with composting, or pruning the one hundred acres of organic vines.

In the early 1990s, Levin and Harman purchased this magnificent all-organic, 160-acre estate that straddles ridges in the Yorkville Highlands AVA with elevations from 1,550 to 1,900 feet. An old stagecoach road that used to connect Ukiah and Boonville crosses through the property. Giant oaks dot the hillsides where sixteen acres of mostly Bordeaux varieties—Cabernet Sauvignon, Merlot, and Cabernet Franc—grow.

"Yorkville Highlands is great for Bordeaux varietals, which ripen at this altitude to make the most intense dark red juice," says Levin, slim and dressed in black jeans, a blanket wool jacket and cowboy boots. To Levin, who became interested in winemaking when he drank first-growth wines from Bordeaux in France, is fulfilling a dream. "I fell in love with Chateau Margaux and wanted to match that quality," he says.

Levin grew up in San Francisco, a young classical musician who became principal cellist in the San Francisco Youth Orchestra. "Now I do Dylanesque folk rock music," he says, adding that this is the year he will get his CD out.

In 1983, Levin started in the wine business as négociant with his father, who was a partner at Zellerbach Winery in McNab Valley just south of Ukiah. When Levin met Harman, she was designing wine labels, which she still does for Le Vin and other wineries.

Harman grew up in San Mateo. When she was in her teens, her mother Gloria met and later married (in 1973) Art Clokey, the creator of the clay animation character Gumby. "I worked on Gumby and Pokey episodes," she says, and designed murals for the fiftieth anniversary celebration in 2006, one of which is on display at the winery.

The winery is housed in a big barn on a knoll. The first floor tasting room with its elbow-high oak bar and stacks of barrels amid artwork is open by appointment only. In addition to their estate Merlot, Cabernet Sauvignon, Cabernet Franc, Syrah and Merlot Ruby Rosé wines, Le Vin makes Pinot Noir grown at Lost Creek Vineyard near Maple Creek Winery. Wine poster artist Steven Haines Hall in Mill Valley inspired their Art Deco label.

Everything is certified organic on the estate. "When chemical fertilizers are used continuously, the soil eventually loses its ability to fix nitrogen, an essential element in vineyards for producing high-quality wine," says Levin. "We add organic compost by hand to each vine and dig it in."

No wonder they subscribe to the WWOOF program. Harman and Levin got involved with the WWOOFers from their connection to the Solar Living Center in Hopland. Harman was doing design work there and met her first WWOOFer interns at the SLC.

Levin, Eric's family name, couldn't have been more appropriate. "As exemplified in the movie, *Bottle Shock*, for years the end all was being French," laughs Levin. "After all, Levin is 'wine' in French. We have name recognition built in."

FETZER AND FAMILY

In 1958, Barney and Kathleen Fetzer purchased their Home Ranch, including a rundown vineyard in Redwood Valley. Ten years later the Fetzers, who had eleven children all raised working in the vineyard and winery, produced their first vintage. Since then, the Fetzer name has become synonymous with high quality and value, as well as organically grown wines from Mendocino. In the 1980s, the Fetzers bought the beautiful Valley Oaks (now Campovida) ranch and built a state-of-the-art winery in Hopland. Fetzer's Valley Oaks was a showcase during the California Cuisine movement. The family grew the winery from 2500 to 2.5 million cases. In the 1990s, under the leadership of winemaker Paul Dolan, Fetzer created the Bonterra brand to showcase their commitment to organically grown grapes. When the Fetzer family sold the winery in 1992, each sibling ended up with a vineyard in Mendocino County. Five of the Fetzers have their own wine labels in Mendocino. In addition Jim Fetzer created Ceago Vinegarden in neighboring Lake County. And the next generation is picking up the torch, each continuing the Fetzer commitment to organic grapes.

FETZER
CHAMPION OF SUSTAINABILITY

SARACINA
HAVEN OF ARTISTIC REYCYCLING

JERIKO
CLAN'S ARTIST IN MEDITERRANEAN VILLA

OSTER FAMILY
BLUEGRASS AND CAB

PATIANNA ORGANIC VINEYARDS
A WAY OF LIFE

MASUT
THE NEXT GENERATION

FETZER
CHAMPION OF SUSTAINABILITY

The seeds of sustainability started at Fetzer in the late 1980s before "green" and "sustainable" were popular terms. Fetzer was one of the first to redesign vineyards to include riparian borders as natural habitat corridors for native wildlife. Cover crops and flowering plants like clovers, bell beans and vetch are planted between vines to enhance soil quality, reduce weeds and keep away harmful insects.

In the 1990s, Fetzer's goal of "zero waste" translated to recycling all used paper, cardboard, glass, plastics and metal and composting the grape stems, seeds and skins. In 2006, Fetzer installed one of the wine industry's largest arrays of solar panels, which is 75,000 square feet in size and generates 899 kilowatts, supplying green power to run the bottling plant.

Fetzer's barrel room was built against an earthen berm. This adds a natural cooling atmosphere and eliminates the need for artificial air conditioning. The administration building was the first commercially built rammed earth construction in Mendocino County. Electric carts carry workers around the grounds. Heavily insulated holding tanks reduce cooling expense. Winery and vineyard workers carpool in vans supplied by Fetzer.

Fetzer published a handbook on growing organic and sustainable winegrapes, which has been distributed widely to growers. In addition to their manager of sustainability, Ann Thrupp, Fetzer has a longtime winemaker and many other employees who are committed to the sustainability mission.

Director of winemaking Dennis Martin oversees six assistant winemakers. Dennis says he strives to continue the style of winemaking that Paul Dolan, now one of the wine industry's foremost leaders in sustainable business and viticulture practices, developed along with Fetzer's founder, Barney Fetzer.

Dennis, who has made wine at Fetzer since the early 1980s, grew up on a ranch in the Central

Valley, where his family raised Thompson seedless grapes as well as peaches, plums and nectarines. He received a degree in Agricultural Business in 1973, and a master's degree in Enology and Food Science in 1975 from California State University at Fresno.

When Dennis was in graduate school at Fresno State, he met Paul Dolan. "Paul was a great mentor," he says.

Fetzer's employees refer to sustainability as "E3" which was coined under the leadership of Paul Dolan and the Fetzer family. It stands equally for environmental, economic and social equity aims. E3 is embraced as an important part of the company's culture, and a cornerstone to the way of doing business.

Fetzer gives E3 awards each year to an employee who comes up with a new sustainability idea or project. One year it went to a backhoe driver who put recycle bins at each building for the employees to compost lunch and snack leftovers. It also has gone to a team of people involved in lightweight bottling innovation. In recent years, the E3 awards have added the name of the late Patrick Healy, in memory of a beloved employee and long time environmental champion.

Fetzer's innovations and awards can be found on the Fetzer Vineyards website along with many details about their wines. Fetzer makes a wine for every taste from the slightly sweet Gewurztraminer and White Zinfandel to the bone dry Sauvignon Blanc and Pinot Grigio to the food friendly Chardonnay and Syrah Rosé. Fetzer Moscato is their sweet dessert wine.

Fetzer's red wines include Syrah, Pinot Noir, Zinfandel, Cabernet Sauvignon and Merlot. The website has an excellent food and wine pairing chart, recipes to go with all the wines, and a summary of the winery's sustainable practices.

In 2011 the Chilean wine company Concha y Toro purchased Fetzer Vineyards. A world-renowned winery, the Guilisasti and Larraín families that own Concha y Toro segued into their first American venture with enthusiasm and commitment to Fetzer's long-standing environmental reputation.

SARACINA

HAVEN OF ARTISTIC RECYCLING

Passersby are drawn by the giant willows weeping in the breeze by the farm pond and a cupola-topped structure next to the cave entrance. Locals are lured by the reputation of Saracina's wines and curiosity about the latest enterprise of the eldest of the Fetzer clan. Adventurers want to tour Mendocino County's first wine caves. These are a snippet of the attractions at Saracina Winery and Vineyards, west of Highway 101 just north of Hopland.

John Fetzer and Patty Rock named their biodiverse ranch Saracina for the place in Tuscany where the couple honeymooned in 1998. "This ranch reminds us of Mediterranean hillsides," says Patty. John's creativity and relentless handiwork create a destination embellished with a mixture of reverence for beauty coupled with recycled practicality.

Focal points along the driveway include a stone outbuilding that looks like an ancient Tuscan fort and groves of gnarled-trunk olive trees transplanted from a hundred-year-old ranch in Corning in California's Central Valley. A forest of golden willows borders the pond and handcrafted iron chairs grace lawns in front of the caves.

John Fetzer's visionary talent started at a young age, growing up the oldest of eleven Fetzer children in Redwood Valley. After the untimely passing of his father Barney Fetzer, the family patriarch and Fetzer winery founder, John became CEO of Fetzer Vineyards at the age of thirty-five.

John has lived on this ranch since 1981 when it was known as Sundial, home of Fetzer's popular Sundial Chardonnay. He maintains a block of Chardonnay for sentimental reasons, but most of the three hundred acres of vineyards are planted in other varietals.

Grapes from Saracina Vineyards and from the Fetzer family home ranch in Redwood Valley go into Saracina and Atrea wines made by John Fetzer and Alex MacGregor. Saracina wines include Syrah, Pinot Noir, Zinfandel and Petite Sirah, as well as Sauvignon Blanc that has a minerally brightness and melon-like aroma.

Atrea's name is a play on the word "atria" for chambers of the heart, says Patty.

"Our wines have and will always be made with the heart and soul of Mendocino in them," adds John. Atrea blends include Old Soul Red and The Choir, named for a spectacular display of art inside the cave.

John says he designed the caves "by the seat of my pants." He knew this hillock was rocky but when they starting boring they found the entire cave would be bored into solid rock. Gunnite covers the interior to keep pieces of the Franciscan shale from shedding. Down a wine barrel-lined passage is a softly lit alcove where the "choir" glows in all its glory. Seventeen six-foot high ceramic artisanal interpretations of antique Chinese wine vessels are topped with rounded ceramic cork-like heads, each shaped with a unique face and together resembling a row of singers.

"We bought them from the contemporary artist Luo Xu after seeing them at his property in China," says Patty. She and John named their Atrea blend of estate-grown Roussanne and Viognier The Choir as homage to the sculptures.

"Our style is a mix of Asian, Italian and Mendocino," says Patty, who grew up in Michigan. She was the chief administrative officer of a law firm in Silicon Valley when she and John met. "I turned in my suits and heels to come to the ranch," she laughs.

John is famous for recycling old building materials. He gathered broken slabs from old concrete driveways to use as stones for patios and walls on the ranch. He once trucked home pieces of a demolished bridge from Covelo in eastern Mendocino County to craft an archway on the highest knoll on the property, superb for its 360-degree view.

"John collects castoffs," says Patty. "I can't just drive by a demolition," John admits.

JERIKO ESTATE

CLAN'S ARTIST IN MEDITERRANEAN VILLA

Artist, architect and youngest son of Mendocino's winegrowing Fetzer clan, Daniel Fetzer created his winery by drawing from what was here and overlaying it with early California, Tuscan and Provençal influences.

The result is Jeriko Estate, a classic Mediterranean compound with adobe colored walls, red tiled roofs and graceful archways on the west side of Highway 101 north of Hopland. The picturesque villa known as the Estate House that sits behind the winery was once a Colonial-style farmhouse. "It was built in 1898 by Judge Sturtevant," says Daniel, who remodeled it a hundred years later. "Colonial and Mediterranean rooflines have similar features," he says "Adding stucco and tile also reflect early California architecture." He applied the same combination to the winery that was once an old prune shed.

"I wanted a new feel for the property," he says. The name Jeriko derives from an ancient civilization. It stands for "city of agriculture," the place where plants and animals were first domesticated along the banks of the Jordan River.

When Daniel took over the ranch he farmed using biodynamic and organic practices. The soil was great, but the vineyards were old and rundown. He replanted all but a thirteen-acre block of Chardonnay next to the Russian River. "The grapes in that block are intensely flavored and we found them perfect for our Brut sparkling wine," he says, adding that Jeriko made America's first organic sparkling wine. Its first vintage, the 2001 Brut, won Best of Show at the prestigious Orange County Wine Competition. Daniel replanted the old vineyards with Pinot Noir, Chardonnay, Merlot, Syrah, and Sangiovese vines.

Inside the tasting room, the light is low so it doesn't interfere with the outside view and with the exposed barrel room on the other side of a glass panel. The handcrafted bar with its large pine farm tables, comfortable chairs and a corner fireplace invite leisurely tasting. Outside, tables in the courtyard are surrounded by olive trees and lavender borders. The setting is perfect for summer weddings and musical concerts. Nearby, the Estate House with six bedrooms, a pool, billiards room and state-of-the-art kitchen is available for rent through Jeriko's website.

The Jeriko label is on Daniel's Sauvignon Blanc, Chardonnay, Pinot Noir, Grenache Noir, Syrah, Merlot, Sangiovese, Cabernet Sauvignon, Rosé, and Brut and Sparkling Rosé wines. In addition, Daniel produces a second brand, San Francisco Wine Press. The label, done in sepia tones with burnished edges and a representation of a lithograph from an 1850 Scientific American magazine, resembles an old newspaper.

"We created a newspaper look in honor of the heritage of the printing press," says Daniel. It is also a tribute to the early immigrants, who carted their grapes from Mendocino, Sonoma and Napa to San Francisco where many of the industry's first wines were made.

Both Jeriko and the San Francisco Press labels honor the Fetzer family history. From his parents' courtship in the Bay Area to their ultimate settling on the 800-acre ranch in Redwood Valley, Daniel Fetzer continues with the family legacy at Jeriko.

OSTER FAMILY
BLUEGRASS AND CABERNET

Music, family and birthright weave into the story of Oster Wine Cellars. This small-town family story begins with Teresa and Ken Oster, who were raised in Redwood Valley, met in kindergarten in Redwood Valley, and now own vineyards and a winery in Redwood Valley. Their grown children, Adrianna and Gibson, are married and live with their spouses in the Valley. Everyone is involved in the vineyard and winery. Their passion is Cabernet Sauvignon from Redwood Valley.

"We are very family oriented," says the personable Teresa, who is the tenth of Barney and Kathleen Fetzer's eleven children. The winery is on a 200-acre property on Tomki Road that was purchased by Ken's parents in 1964. His mom June lives in a 1920s bungalow on what was once the old Williams ranch.

A fourth generation grape grower, Ken grew up under these giant oaks and evergreens among farm animals and vineyards. "My family grew grapes near Cloverdale," he says. "We just recently found a receipt from 1894 for wine grapes sold to the old Italian Swiss Colony in Asti." Before becoming a full time grape grower and part time guitar maker, Ken got into metal fabrication and had his own portable welding and steel business. "I can fix anything that isn't electronic," he laughs.

Teresa grew up on the west side of Redwood Valley at the Fetzer family home ranch. From an early age, she worked labeling and bottling at Fetzer Vineyards. She remembers when "we kids were put in charge of these gigantic tasks."

Although schoolmates since kindergarten, Teresa and Ken didn't become attracted to each other until they were sophomores in high school. "There is nothing like falling in love with my best friend's sister," says Ken. They were married in 1979.

In 1992, when the family sold Fetzer and the vineyard properties were divided among the siblings, Ken and Teresa became full-time farmers. They sell most of their all-organic Cabernet Sauvignon and Merlot grapes to local wineries.

The Osters launched their own wine brand in 2002 with the goal to make an ultra premium Cabernet Sauvignon. These grapes grow especially well on their site in Redwood Valley. Adrianna Gozza, who is the winemaker, says, "We want to express the beautifully unique terroir of the Redwood

Valley Appellation, this place we are so lucky to call home." They market several hundred cases to their wine club members.

Adrianna, an assistant winemaker at Roederer Estate, has a master's degree in viticulture and enology from UC Davis. She's worked at other Fetzer family-owned wineries including Uncle Dan's Jeriko, Uncle John's Saracina and Uncle Jim's Ceago. Her husband Joe Gozza is a vineyard manager for Chevalier Vineyard Management Inc. Her brother Gibson manages the family vineyards.

A beautiful redwood barn houses the winery where barrels line the walls. Oster Cabernet is fermented with native yeast and not filtered, just fined. It spends eighteen months in the barrel and has one year of bottle aging before being released. "It is a classic Cabernet Sauvignon blended with Merlot," says Adrianna.

Oster's label, shaped like a guitar pick, reflects the family's love of music. Ken, who builds guitars and repairs mandolins and guitars, has played bluegrass since he was a kid. Adrianna plays the standup bass and sings. They have a family band with local friends called Grassfire. Their winery events such as for A Taste of Redwood Valley are focused around bluegrass music, says Teresa. "We do everything here, and everyone is involved in every facet," says Teresa. And they do it all with music.

PATIANNA ORGANIC VINEYARDS
A WAY OF LIFE

Biodiversity at Patianna Organic Vineyards, along Old River Road north of Hopland, is apparent at first sight. Chickens scratch between grape vines. Goats nibble in riparian borders. Remains of pesky rodents pile up under owl boxes. Piles of organic matter and manure decompose into soil enrichments. Biodynamic and organic describe Patianna's operation and owner Patti Fetzer's lifestyle.

The fifth of the eleven Fetzer children from Mendocino County's renowned Fetzer family, Patti grew up in the vineyard. "I was five when we moved to the family ranch in Redwood Valley," she says. "As soon as any of us was tall enough to reach the vines we learned to sucker and thin."

She laughs at the memory of a story her dad Barney liked to share. When he told folks he had eleven children and they asked if he had a football team, he would pause and say, "No, I have a wine team!" Everyone found their niche in the family-run business and Patti Fetzer was one of the artists. She designed the wine labels and was in charge of all package design for the different Fetzer labels as well as point of sale pieces.

The family sold Fetzer winery in 1992. Six years later they divided the vineyards among the family members and Patti Fetzer became proprietor of this 126-acre former pear ranch now known as Patianna.

The name Patianna comes from Patti's name Patricia Ann, "with a bit of Italian accent on my German heritage," she laughs. Her husband Gregg Hileman, a chef who cooked at the former Fetzer Valley Oaks Hospitality Center (now Campovida), is Patianna's general manager.

Their 75 acres of Chardonnay and Sauvignon Blanc vineyards are Demeter Certified Biodynamic®. Ranch foreman Horacio Ortega has tended the grapes on this ranch for more than twenty-five years. He grew up in Cerro Colorado, Michoacán, Mexico, where his father was a farmer. Horacio and his wife Lorena live on the ranch with their children. He became a

United States citizen the same year Patianna became Demeter Certified Biodynamic®.

To diversify the ranch's habitat, Patti and Horacio fenced areas and brought in sheep and goats that eat down the foliage where such threats to grapevines as glassy-winged sharpshooters like to breed. The chickens, which spend the night in a coop on wheels that is moved around the vineyard, are also in the vineyard for a purpose. "We had cutworms," says Horacio, "and now we don't because they scratch under the vines, keeping bugs, insects and weeds away." Patti adds, "and they lay the most wonderful eggs with orange yolks."

Patti describes their estate-grown wine as "fruit forward with no oak." Patianna Chardonnay and Sauvignon Blanc are all fermented in stainless steel. Their Syrah comes from Julie and Joe Golden's Fairbairn Ranch in Hopland.

Several of Patti's siblings have property adjacent or nearby and gather for family picnics regularly on the wide bank of the Russian River. A tangle of blackberries separates the vineyard from the riverfront. Patti says her mom taught her how to bake and she makes cobblers from the berries. "I get a lot of pleasure from this lifestyle," she says and credits her upbringing for her respect for the land. "My mother taught us to put things back better than we found them. Mother Nature deserves the same."

MASUT
THE NEXT GENERATION

Continuing their Mendocino family's winemaking tradition is so important to Jacob and Benjamin Fetzer they added the words "third generation" to their Masut wine label and business cards.

Their grandfather, the late Barney Fetzer, was one of Mendocino County's trailblazing vintners. The two brothers grew up next door to Barney on the Fetzer family's Redwood Valley home ranch. Now Jake and Ben make wine from the grapes they helped their late dad Bobby Fetzer plant when they were in high school.

"It was natural for dad to buy this piece of property," says Ben. The 1500-acre ranch butts up to the home ranch. Growing up, Bobby Fetzer and some of his ten siblings "trespassed to go hiking" on the steep canyons of what was then a neighboring property.

Bobby, along with his wife and the boys' mom Sheila, purchased the ranch in 1992 after the Fetzer family sold their Hopland-based winery. They named the ranch Masut, a Pomo word for dark, rich earth and for a former Pomo settlement in the area.

Their dad's love of farming and restoring old ranches was passed on to Jake and Ben. The beautiful barn that the brothers have partitioned for the winery offices and storage just off of Highway 101 was built of recycled redwood, as was a five thousand square foot barn with a dirt floor that sits on a knoll with a 360-degree view.

Bobby and Sheila planted a vineyard on the ranch with Pinot Noir, "Dad's favorite wine." In the meantime Ben and Jake went off to college. Jake studied business at Fort Lewis College in Durango, Colorado. Ben went to Lewis and Clark in Oregon and to Chico. The brothers always knew they would come back to the ranch.

"When our parents bought a 6000-acre ranch in Covelo where we raise organic cattle and hay, I stayed here to farm the vineyard," says Jake. Ben moved to Covelo to help with the cattle.

Everything is organic, a tradition the Fetzer brothers continue from their family commitment. When they decided to make wine, they finished the inside of the hilltop barn creating a state-of-the-art winery. Inside the rustic redwood-sided barn with the green metal roof they make Pinot Noir in the Burgundian-style.. That means, for one thing, they finish fermentation inside the barrel. Until April, the wine is left *sur lie*, which means in contact with the spent yeast. "*Sur lie* creates more complexity and depth and acts as an antioxidant," adds Jake.

They credit esteemed winemaker Greg LaFollette, their friend and mentor, for his advice and tasting expertise and for the immediate accolades their first release received.

"We do hands-on farming, beef growing, winemaking and marketing," says Jake, adding, "when you like to do things yourself, it's easier to control quality. We have our handprints on every bottle."

"We are finding a lot more to do at Masut than ranching, especially now that we are making wine," says Ben. "We also build fences, fix drip irrigation systems, and deal with wine distributors."

Jake and Ben dedicated their 2009 Masut inaugural Pinot Noir to their dad Bobby Fetzer. "Our dad and our mom taught us how to live and work on a ranch," says Jake. Ben and Jake agree that the biggest thing about their lives is their family heritage. "It's why we are here."

PUTTING
ANDERSON VALLEY
ON THE MAP

Anderson Valley, named for Walter Anderson, the first European to settle here in 1851, stretches for thirty-five miles along Highway 128, a scenic drive between the Redwood and Coast highways. This bucolic valley led the way for the growth of Mendocino's contemporary wine reputation. World-class Pinot Noir comes from here; as do Alsatian-style grapes, such as Riesling and Gewurztraminer that thrive in the fog-cooled climate so close to the coast. Then there is the méthode champenoise sparkling wine made from Pinot Noir and Chardonnay grapes. Additionally, acres of recently planted olive trees grown by farmers to diversify and capitalize on a crop with growing market value, adjoin antique apple orchards and historic sheep ranches along the way. The six wineries in this section helped grow the popularity and renown of Anderson Valley wines. The story spans the decades beginning in the late 1960s and the 1970s with Lazy Creek, Husch, Edmeades (owned by Kendall Jackson in Sonoma County) and Navarro Vineyards. It continues with Handley, Scharffenberger and Greenwood Ridge and moves forward with Zina Hyde Cunningham. For a list of Anderson Valley wineries please refer to the Wine Routes section and see the map at the back of this book.

NAVARRO VINEYARDS
ALSATIAN VARIETALS AND ICONIC WINERY

HANDLEY CELLARS
WINE, FOOD AND FOLK ART

SCHARFFENBERGER CELLARS
MENDOCINO'S HOUSE BUBBLY

GREENWOOD RIDGE
BASEBALL, COLLECTIONS AND ARCHITECTURE

ZINA HYDE CUNNINGHAM
BOONVILLE DESTINATION

Navarro Vineyards

Alsatian Varietals and Iconic Winery

Navarro Vineyards is an Anderson Valley icon. Surrounded by vineyards, well-groomed gardens and shaded picnic tables, the charming redwood tasting room is one of the busiest in Mendocino County. Navarro is the standard bearer of American Alsatian-style wines such as Gewurztraminer and Riesling. Navarro Pinot Noir is rated among the best around. As the first winery to develop direct marketing to the public, Navarro sells ninety percent of their wine in the tasting room and through their wine club and newsletter. Navarro Vineyards is the oldest continuously operating winery in Anderson Valley.

Prior to moving to Anderson Valley in the 1970s, Ted Bennett and Deborah Cahn were already "wine geeks." They were passionate about the wines of Alsace and decided they would find the perfect place to grow Gewurztraminer. Ted had just sold Pacific Stereo, a successful Bay Area-based company.

Ted and Deborah looked at vineyards in various parts of the state and found that in many places Gewurztraminer ripened too soon or too quickly to develop the intense flavor the grape is known for in Alsace. "The great wines of Europe develop because the grapes struggle to get ripe," says Ted.

Then in October 1972, Deborah and Ted had an opportunity to pick Gewurztraminer grapes on a rainy day at Edmeades Winery in Anderson Valley. "We were picking and sloshing through the mud and finding the grape flavors were really intense. Just what we were looking for," says Ted. "So we bought the place across the road."

Describing themselves as part of the back-to-the-land movement of the 1970s, Deborah explains that coming from Berkeley she had a romantic vision of social change, but was also a realist. "I realized I couldn't change the whole world, but I can control what happens in my own corner."

Over the years they developed their specific areas of specialty. Deborah describes her role as "language." She writes Navarro's popular newsletter, which is like receiving a taste of Navarro at home, filled with stories about the people and the wines. Ted is the "hands-on energy." They both confer on blending with their long time winemaker Jim Klein.

Deborah and Ted focused on Alsatian varietals not only because they like them, but also for marketing reasons. At the time, Chardonnay and Cabernet Sauvignon were so popular, wineries were competing for the same customers. "We became a big fish in a small pond by increasing interest in Riesling and dry-style Gewurztraminer," says Deborah.

I REALIZED I COULDN'T CHANGE THE WHOLE WORLD BUT I CAN CONTROL WHAT HAPPENS IN MY OWN CORNER.

—DEBORAH CAHN,
NAVARRO VINEYARDS

"Gewurztraminer is a hard sell," adds Ted. He credits Navarro's successes to developing their customer-driven business model. "People come into the tasting room, try one of our wines and come back year after year to buy more."

Their children Aaron and Sarah, were born and raised in Anderson Valley, went off to college, and returned to work as partners in the business. Aaron is Navarro's webmaster, while Sarah is involved in winemaking at Navarro and also oversees the family's organic vineyard outside of Boonville. Sarah has a flock of chickens, keeps a bunch of Baby Doll sheep, which mow the winter grass between the vines, and manages a herd of seventy-five goats to provide milk for her small cheese dairy.

In addition to the Alsatian varietals and Pinot Noir, Chardonnay, Pinot Gris and Muscat grapes grown on their ninety acres of vineyards, Navarro makes Old Vine Cuvée Zinfandel from a couple of Ukiah Valley vineyards. One is the Tollini family where the Zinfandel was planted in the 1930s. The other is Cononiah, owned by the Berry family in Talmage, which has vines planted in the 1940s. Navarro sources Zinfandel from thirty-year-old Eaglepoint Vineyards vines. Their Chenin Blanc comes from fourth generation Redwood Valley grapegrowers John and Michelle Young.

"We enjoy dealing with the old family vineyard owners in Ukiah," says Ted. "I like doing business with the old timers and their families because they know what it's like to farm—they have experience with the cycles of highs and lows. Unlike in the corporate world where I came from, where you look for someone to blame when things go wrong, in farming weather and nature rule. You have no control and they are greater than you are."

Handley Cellars
Wine, Food and Folk Art

A Mendocino wine and international culinary adventure begins in Handley Cellars' tasting room. Not only does Milla Handley make wine that complements courses from appetizers through dessert, her wines are also compatible with many ethnic cuisines. One look around the tasting room at the extensive collection of African, Asian, South Pacific Island and Latin American folk art and you can imagine the possibilities.

Handley's carefully crafted wines, which range from Gewurztraminer to Chardonnay, Pinot Noir to Zinfandel, Water Tower White to Estate Brut sparkling wine, have recipes to go with them. While tasting, you can browse through the recipes on the beautifully carved, old English pub bar.

"Our food and wine pairings and the design on our wine label are inspired by the indigenous art collected by my parents from around the world," says Milla. Her father, the late Raymond Handley, founded the gallery Xanadu, located in a Frank Lloyd Wright building in San Francisco.

As the great-granddaughter of Henry Weinhard, one of the original brewmasters of Oregon, Milla inherited her interest in fermentation. In 1975,

she was one of the first women to receive a degree in fermentation science from the University of California at Davis. After graduation, she worked with Richard Arrowood at Chateau St. Jean in Sonoma Valley. In 1978, Milla and her late husband, Rex McClellan, moved to Anderson Valley.

She started out working with Lake County wine-maker Jed Steele, who was then at Edmeades Winery in Anderson Valley. "I figured out pretty soon that I wanted to have my own place," says Milla.

In 1982 she established Handley Cellars. The winery is located on an old sheep ranch on Highway 128, northwest of Philo. The ranch house with its wraparound porch has been meticulously restored and is used for special events. A water tower and restored barn are among the historic buildings.

The gate at the entrance to Handley Cellars is the first sign of the artwork to come. The diagonal block design, also represented on Handley's wine label, was inspired by ancient textiles of the Shoowa tribe from the ancient Kuba kingdom in central Africa. On the first weekend of the month, the entrance flag announces a culinary adventure.

Inside the tasting room, the hand carved teak elephant chairs and table catch the eye. Textiles, jewelry and garden sculptures from Indonesia and the Middle East set the scene. On the culinary adventure weekends and at their special events, Handley pairs a featured wine with a food sampling. Recent examples include Chardonnay with Indonesian fish curry, Pinot Noir and Indian masala-spiced duck, and Syrah with Chinese five-spiced short ribs.

"Every day, every hour is different," she says, "no matter how much wine you produce." Milla is a hands-on winemaker. When she isn't out selling wine, she is holding court in her office, checking on the tasting room, driving a forklift, testing grape sugars, tasting barrel samples and being managed by her creative and energetic staff. She and her late husband raised two daughters, Megan Warren, an attorney, and Lulu, a graduate of UC Berkeley.

The winery, tasting room and ranch house are surrounded by twenty-eight acres of certified organic vineyards. Most are planted to Pinot Noir, but there are also eight-plus acres of Chardonnay and five acres of Gewurztraminer, the spicy aromatic grape that goes so wonderfully with Thai curry and Mexican carnitas. "Our Gewurztraminer is pretty dry with just a hint of sweetness," says Milla. Handley also makes Pinot Gris and Riesling, which, along with Gewurztraminer, are Alsatian varietals that grow well in Anderson Valley.

Although only produced every three years, one of Milla Handley's loves is sparkling wine, made in the méthode champenoise of French Champagne. The results are creamy with tight, tiny bubbles and European-style aromas and flavors, an easy wine to choose for any cuisine.

SCHARFFENBERGER CELLARS
MENDOCINO'S HOUSE BUBBLY

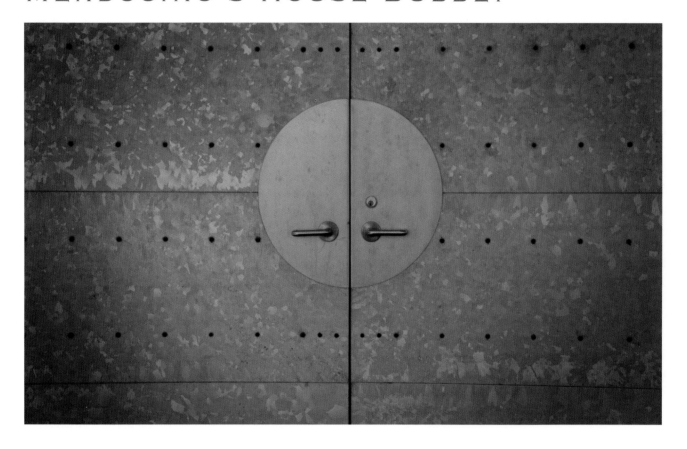

When John Scharffenberger began Scharffenberger Cellars in 1981 in Anderson Valley, he was the first commercial producer of méthode champenoise sparkling wine in Mendocino County, with all of his grapes coming from Anderson Valley.

Scharffenberger's tasting room is in a Mendocino country bungalow in downtown Philo. Behind it, the 35,000-square-foot winery is a grandly scaled yet graceful structure, sitting between valley and hillside vineyards. Riveted metal doors and the sandblasted glass entry add local artisan touches. An old redwood grove has been carefully protected on the 160-acre property.

Tex Sawyer, the winemaker, has shepherded the making of Scharffenberger Cellars' sparkling wines since 1989. The native Texan supervises the production, from harvest through two fermentation processes, to produce a unique American-style sparkling wine.

Drawn to the wine industry, Tex got a job in 1979 at Navarro Vineyards and discovered Anderson Valley. A year later he met his wife Lynne and by 1989 they had two sons, were living in Anderson Valley and he was winemaker at Scharffenberger.

Scharffenberger's sparkling wine blend is made from approximately sixty-five percent Pinot Noir and thirty-five percent Chardonnay grapes. Scharffenberger Brut goes through malolactic fermentation. In this process, a malolactic strain of bacteria is added to the wine to produce a creamy texture and finish.

In addition to Brut, Brut Rosé, Cremant and the occasional vintage reserve-quality Blanc de Blancs (all Chardonnay), Scharffenberger wines also include nonsparkling varietals such as Pinot Noir, Syrah, Pinot Gris and Chardonnay, which are sold only in the tasting room.

Known for its exhibits by local artists, Scharffenberger's tasting room is a hub of conviviality when each new show begins with a Friday night reception.

Scharffenberger Cellars has been owned since 2004 by Maisons Marques & Domaines, the American arm of Champagne Louis Roederer. If sparkling wine seems like a special occasion wine, a stop at the tasting room will dispel that myth. As Mendocino's house bubbly, Scharffenberger Brut and Brut Rosé are household staples, a practice approved by Tex.

"The bottom line is that it's always okay to keep a bottle of sparkling wine in the fridge," says Tex, who enjoys life in Anderson Valley paired with a daily dose of sparkling wine.

GREENWOOD RIDGE

BASEBALL, COLLECTIONS AND ARCHITECTURE

Before describing Greenwood Ridge tasting room's Frank Lloyd Wright-inspired architecture, the wines, the wine-can collection, the line of screw-cap varietals, the silkscreened labels and the annual California Wine Tasting Championships, the operating word here is … baseball.

Proprietor and winemaker Allan Green is tall and athletic with a passion for America's favorite pastime. He plays centerfield for the Greenwood Ridge Dragons, a team he formed in 2001 made up of players mostly from Mendocino and Sonoma counties. The Dragons, who play in the fifty-five-and-over division in the Redwood Empire Baseball League and in the Men's Senior Baseball League tournament in Arizona, have won the title to the over-fifty World Championships over and over again. They've also won the over-fifty-two championship in Florida. Their season

begins in the spring after pruning and ends just before harvest, hopefully.

Allan Green found winemaking through his love of baseball. In 1973, his family purchased vineyards on Greenwood Ridge. Four years later, Allan, an artist, designer, music buff and wine and beer can collector, moved from Los Altos to the ranch. He began playing softball in Anderson Valley with teammates who were guys working in Anderson Valley's fledgling wine industry. "I got into this business because I like living here," Allan says, with a laugh.

Allan began making wine in 1980. His first release was a White Riesling, which is still one of Greenwood Ridge's benchmark wines.

In the 1980s, Allan acquired the seven-acre triangle along Highway 128 just west of Philo and built his distinctive octagonal tasting room, designed by his father, Aaron Green, an associate of Frank Lloyd Wright. It was built from wood milled from a single redwood tree that had fallen on the family's Greenwood Ridge Ranch in the 1960s. Solar panels installed in 2005 provide all the power for the tasting room. Picnic tables amid native vegetation, and an arched bridge to an island in the middle of the pond, add a welcoming environment where wine tasters can be found picnicking, even in the winter.

From the tasting room windows, views encompass the surrounding vineyards, from the row of deciduous poplars to the rolling hills. Inside, an octagonal glass case displays dozens of wine cans from Green's extensive collection. Some of the cans, with names like Vin-Tin-Age, Bigatti Vino and Apple Splitz, date to the 1930s. Newer additions are in sleek 750ml recyclable cans.

All of Greenwood Ridge's wine is labeled with a dramatic, fire-breathing, long-tailed dragon, silkscreened on each bottle. This label has a Frank Lloyd Wright connection. In 1959, Green's father gave a cast-iron dragon fountain to the Frank Lloyd Wright Foundation. Mrs. Wright, however, preferred that the dragon be fire-breathing rather than water-spouting. She added a discreetly placed propane tank; the dragon is on display at Taliesin West in Scottsdale, Arizona.

Another innovation at Greenwood Ridge is the screw cap. Following the lead of ninety percent of

New Zealand's wineries, Green did a test run of screw caps and was so impressed at the consistency and quality that he converted from corks.

Greenwood Ridge wine are made from grapes grown on Allan's ranch that is within America's only noncontiguous American Viticultural Area (AVA) known as Mendocino Ridge. All AVAs are designated because of their unique geographic, climatic and other ecological characteristics. Mendocino Ridge AVA, established in 1997, is composed of a series of ridgetop vineyards above the fog line, known as "islands in the sky."

Allan plays his wine and baseball doubleheader all year. His wines range from the fruity aromatic Riesling and Sauvignon Blanc to classic Merlot and Zinfandel. He makes a couple of Zinfandel and Merlot blends: one is Mendovino and the other is….Home Run Red.

ZINA HYDE CUNNINGHAM
A BOONVILLE DESTINATION

Between the Boonville General Store and an antique cherry red pickup loaded with wine barrels is a tasting room like no other in Mendocino County. Oversized handcrafted oak doors lead into Zina Hyde Cunningham. The lavish contemporary Victorian interior includes historical references to a Mendocino family's history.

A beautifully crafted bar with a pressed copper top lines one wall. On another is a marble and oak fireplace flanked with easy chairs and a sofa. You may bring your tasting glass, sit and enjoy the spacious surroundings and architectural accoutrements and watch a video about the winery. The screen is behind the portrait of patriarch Zina Hyde, which hangs over the fireplace.

One of Zina Hyde's descendants, great-great-grandson Steve Ledson, is the co-owner of the winery. Steve also owns Ledson Winery in Sonoma Valley, and the Ledson Hotel in the town of Sonoma.

Zina Hyde Cunningham came to California from Maine when he was seventeen years old to join the Gold Rush. Not finding the riches he sought, he settled in San Francisco and started a blacksmith shop. When he had to sell the land to make way for the Palace Hotel, he headed north to Sonoma County. In 1859 Zina Hyde bought a ranch in Windsor and planted Alicante and Zinfandel grapes. By 1862, he was making 8,000 gallons of wine.

Three years later, he visited cousins in Mendocino County and fell in love with the land. The

Cunninghams moved north, planting more Alicante and Zinfandel in Mendocino County. Today, the family continues to grow grapes and farm orchards in both Sonoma and Mendocino Counties.

Another Zina Hyde Cunningham descendant was Steve Ledsen's cousin, the late Bill Cunningham, an educator and school superintendent in Northern California. With Bill's inspiration and Steve's contracting know-how, the two decided to re-open the family winery in Mendocino County, and chose Boonville as their new home.

In 2006, Bill and Steve opened Zina Hyde Cunningham tasting room, featuring wine made from Mendocino grapes, just as their great-grandfather had done 150 years earlier.

One of their blends, California Veola is named after Zina Hyde Cunningham's granddaughter. Veola liked to help her father, William Cunningham, with the vineyard and loved Petite Sirah so he planted it. When she tasted the wine it was "too heavy," recounts

the family, so they blended it with Zinfandel and it became her favorite. When she died, her family continued making the 50/50 blend of Petite Sirah and Zinfandel in honor of Veola.

Other Zina Hyde Cunningham wines include Sauvignon Blanc, Chardonnay, Gewurztraminer and Riesling, Orange Muscat, Carignane and Zinfandel, all from Mendocino County grapes. Their Merlot, Malbec and Cabernet Sauvignon are grown in Lake County.

On a nice day, you can take your tasting glass out one of the six French doors that make up the east wall of the tasting room. Whether outside with the view of golden eastern hillsides, inside the private tasting room, or in front of the fireplace, Zina Hyde Cunningham is a Boonville destination.

Rooted in Mendocino

Beginning with the story of John Parducci, Mendocino's wine patriarch—known as "Mr. Mendocino" and now a partner with his grandson at McNab Ridge Winery—the tales in this section zig zag through some of the many historical figures who are deeply rooted in ths place we call Mendocino. The stories are of everyday farmers and exemplify their spirit and work ethic, each drawn significantly to the land by their fore-fathers and -mothers. Many wineries deserve a place in this section. One that needs mentioning, which is not profiled here but is also rooted in Mendocino's winemaking story, is Whaler Vineyards, owned by Russ and Annie Nyborg, located on Old River Road north of Hopland.

McNab Ridge Winery
Parducci Family Legacy

Silversmith
Patience and Polish

Shandel's Oppenlander
Vines and Heavy Metal

Nelson Vineyards
Blend of Old and New

McNab Ridge Winery

Parducci Family Legacy

Rich Parducci, grandson of Mendocino County's winemaking patriarch, John Parducci, is at ease continuing the family legacy at McNab Ridge Winery in McNab Valley, with his own style.

"I started working the bottling line at Parducci when I was twelve," says Rich. At the time, his grandfather John was the winemaker and his uncle George was the manager of the winery, which was founded in 1932 by great-grandfather, Adolph Parducci.

Adolph came to America from Tuscany when he was sixteen years old. His first winery was in Cloverdale, but a fire, and then Prohibition closed it down. Undaunted, he bought property in Mendocino County in 1921 and planted vineyards on the ranch he purchased in the western foothills north of Ukiah.

In 1931, signs pointed to the end of Prohibition and Adolph began construction of his winery.

It was ready to open at the end of 1933 when Prohibition was repealed. Adolph, John and George brought in 20,000-gallon all-redwood tanks that that are in use today at Parducci, which is now owned by the Thornhill family.

In the 1990s, already in his eighties, John Parducci, no longer at his namesake winery, formed a partnership and purchased the former Zellerbach winery in McNab Valley. He and Rich began making McNab Ridge wines. "Grandpa knew McNab Valley really well. It was where he went hunting over the years," says Rich.

The valley is named for Alexander McNab, a sheep rancher who emigrated from Scotland in the 1860s. He brought with him a couple of border collies and bred them with other sheep dogs, which became a breed, unique to the area, the McNab Shepherd. In honor of the breed and the winery's resident McNab Shepherd, Rich named a red wine blend Fred's Red, and created a label with the dog's likeness.

The Parducci family's favorite wine is Petite Sirah. It's made into a big, bold, jammy mouthful. Rich says Petite Sirah has been a staple at dinner on his grandparents' table as long as he can remember.

"Personally, I like Zinfandel," says Rich. He makes several separate Zinfandel bottlings. One of the most fun is Zinzilla, which he describes as "a California monster Zinfandel." The label features a cartoonlike Zinfandel vine rising out of spooky vineyards under a full moon "wreaking havoc on vines that aren't Zinfandel," he laughs, adding, "It's pretty popular around Halloween."

McNab makes a Cononiah vineyard designated Zinfandel, a Mendocino County Zinfandel and, for the Ohio market, Zincinatti. McNab also produces Coro Mendocino, which is slightly over fifty percent Zinfandel.

McNab was the first Mendocino County winery to produce the South African varietal Pinotage, which grows at the neighboring Napoli ranch. Pinotage came about in the 1920s when South African vintners crossed "the finicky Pinot Noir with the more hearty Cinsault" says Rich, "making a delicious, earthy, fruit-forward flavor that people love."

Port is another family tradition that McNab Ridge is continuing. John Parducci made port for decades and McNab Ridge has a bounteous Zinfandel Port.

McNab Ridge's tasting room is located in downtown Hopland. Known for great food at events such as the spring and fall Hopland Passports, McNab carries the tradition forward for the Mendocino Parducci legacy. Rich's grandfather, "Mr. Mendocino" John Parducci himself, gives his blessing, "Rich has a good personality and is very cooperative with my growers."

SILVERSMITH
PATIENCE AND POLISH

Silversmith Vineyard and Winery belongs to a family that has been raising grapes for six generations. All red, the Zinfandel, Cabernet Sauvignon and Petite Sirah wines are tended, shaped and finished with the same craftsmanship as their namesake, an Irish American silversmith.

Tom's great-grandfather Patrick Cunningham came to America from Ireland in the 1840s. "Just like kids today come from Mexico to find a better life and send money home, my great-granddad's family was beset by the troubles of the potato famine. He was sent to Boston to find work and send money

home," says Tom. His great-grandfather, seeing "Irish need not apply" signs in shop windows had a hard time finding a job.

Cunningham had the good fortune to meet two brothers who, according to family history, were descendants of Paul Revere. They trained him to be a silversmith. When it was time to marry, Cunningham returned to Ireland and brought his bride Maria back

to New York, where he continued as a silversmith. When San Francisco's famed Shreve Jewelers lost their silversmiths to the gold mines, they "raided" New York's silversmiths and Cunningham found himself and his family moving to San Francisco and working at Shreve's.

The Cunninghams had nine children. When one was nearly run over by a horse-drawn cart, Patrick, who had grown up on an Irish farm, decided it was time to move to the country. He took the ferry across the Bay and a train to Windsor where he bought 160 acres near the railroad crossing and the old highway. He relocated his family to the property and planted hops. One of his daughters Catherine, who was born in Windsor, was three when Patrick moved everyone to Ukiah in 1873.

The Cunninghams purchased a ranch from Tom Thomas and began what was to become a friendship with the Thomas family, which has passed from generation to generation and continues to this day. They all grew hops and pears and a few grapes as well.

On the Johnson side of the family, Tom's grandfather, Burt Johnson, came from Oregon where he was in the sheep business. On a sheep-selling trip he met Catherine Cunningham. After they married he bought his first ranch at the old stage stop in Willits.

Catherine preferred city living. She and Burt purchased ranches in Redwood Valley and Ukiah and lived in town. Tom's father, John, was the youngest of Burt and Cate's children. Tom grew up on the farm, went to college at St. Mary's and law school at McGeorge University before moving back to Ukiah. In 1980, he purchased a twenty-acre ranch with thirteen acres in Zinfandel in Redwood Valley. In the mid-1990s, Tom started making bulk wine from his grapes. "The bulk market was really good at the time," he says. Then he started making his own Zinfandel under the Silversmith brand and "one thing led to another."

"Piece by piece, bottle by bottle, case by case," is how Tom Johnson describes building Silversmith Winery and his tasting room alongside Highway 101 in Redwood Valley. He and his wife Debbie are both longtime lawyers in Ukiah.

In addition to the Silversmith label, which includes Zinfandel, Petite Sirah and Cabernet Sauvignon wines, Tom has a second label, Goose and Toad. He also produces wine labeled El Primer Milagro for Hispanic restaurants.

The tasting room ambience is low-key, reflecting the personalities of Tom, who still practices law from a small adjacent office, and Debbie, who is responsible for the giant flowers and pumpkins growing in galvanized tubs around the tasting room and winery.

"It's tough to find a place more beautiful and a job more rewarding," says Tom.

SHANDEL'S OPPENLANDER
VINES AND HEAVY METAL

The Shandel family's Oppenlander Ranch produces some of Mendocino County's most coveted Pinot Noir grapes. Set in Surprise Valley, eight miles from the coast (fifteen miles by road), the pristine Pinot Noir vineyard stretches in neat rows contouring northwest to southeast along the hillside.

Driving into Surprise Valley, less than a mile from the hamlet of Comptche and located about thirty-five miles west of Ukiah, you come into vast clearing surrounded by giant conifers. After rumbling over the cattle grate onto the ranch driveway, an eye-popping compilation of old trucks, rusty metal, tractors and cars of many makes and models appears. Further on there's a mountain of deer antlers, remains of an old dump, and ultimately a family history encompassing more than one hundred years in this spectacular setting.

"I've been here more than sixty years; moved here when I was nine," says Bill Shandel. Bill and his wife Wanda, and his brother Norman and wife Kitty, live in two historic residences on the property.

The old farmhouse, built in the mid-nineteenth century, is one of the oldest log houses in Mendocino County. Bill and Norman's great grandfather, Charles Oppenlander, emigrated from Denmark in the 1860s, arriving in Mendocino County via Australia where he had gone for the Gold Rush. "When great-grandpa came here, he went to work for a railroad tie contractor as the livestock manager and he raised cattle," says Bill. While working in the woods he found this natural opening that was called a prairie in those days, according to the Shandels.

In 1947, when Charles' son William Oppenheimer died, the Shandel brothers and their siblings and mother moved into the home where Bill now lives. The ranch along the north fork of the Albion River encompasses 400 acres on the eastern side of the valley. Three hundred of the acres are in timber management.

Eighteen acres are in vines: sixteen in Pinot Noir and two in Chardonnay. Looking for another way to make a living on the land, Bill, who doesn't drink wine, had a hunch about growing grapes in this valley. "In my heart I knew Pinot Noir would grow," he says. He also admits that he wanted to increase the value of the property and hopefully convince the next generation to keep it.

The Shandel brothers are big men, secure in themselves and hard working. For forty years, Norman was Paul Bunyan for the annual Paul Bunyan Days weekend in Fort Bragg. From an early age, both Bill and Norman worked as loggers and ran a junkyard that took machines, cars and heavy equipment. "We also raise about thirty head of cattle," says Bill.

The brothers planted the vineyard in 1998. "I've had the grape bug since the late 1960s," says Bill. "We initially made wine to show what our vineyard is capable of," says Bill. Their first wine, a 2002 Pinot Noir, surprised the local wine community by winning a double gold at the Mendocino County Fair Wine Competition.

With their first wine, the Shandels started a tradition of releasing their new vintage at the Comptche Volunteer Fire Department Chicken BBQ on Father's Day. "I pour samples of the vintage and donate six cases to the fire department to play with," he says. The Shandels are also supporters of the California Deer Association and the Wild Turkey Federation.

Taking the high road above the sloping vineyard, we stop to view the property. Rusty barrels dot the pastures, bordered with sunken pickups, a '60s-era Chevy, a '70 Dodge and a Model A truck. More collected equipment and vehicles surround the horse barn, outbuildings and aging homes, stretching densely along the driveway like rusty eclectic village.

Five generations have made their living here, shifting focus with the times as need and demand arose. "It's been a great go so far," says Bill.

NELSON FAMILY VINEYARDS
BLEND OF OLD AND NEW

An old wagon wheel hangs over the stuccoed fireplace in the Nelson Family Vineyards tasting room. A grove of redwoods planted in 1933 shades the dance floor. Vineyards next to the popular strawberry stand on Highway 101 just south of Ukiah are on their way to organic certification. Canola grown in an old Carignane vineyard block is harvested for biodiesel for the farm's tractors.

Known for growing excellent grapes since the 1970s, Nelson Family Vineyards has been home to Greg Nelson since he was five years old. In 1951, his father Herman and mother Clara purchased the old sheep and pear ranch that was once part of a Mexican land grant, and moved the family from Evergreen near San Jose to Ukiah Valley.

"My parents had grown apricots and prunes and knew nothing about wine grapes," Nelson recalls. "At first they pruned the few acres of grapes on the ranch like they were fruit trees, but they quickly changed that practice."

Today, 180 acres of grapes grow on the ranch and there are still 30 acres of pears. The Nelsons have a forest of cut-your-own Christmas trees, ten acres leased for strawberries, an olive orchard and they lease acreage for cattle to range.

Priding themselves on sustainability, the Nelsons spread compost mulch between the vines to enhance the soil and inhibit weed growth. Their sheep graze in the hillside Cabernet vineyard until bud break. Riparian borders are lush along the creek. Drainage ditches that used to be V shaped allowing dirty runoff are sculpted into wide plains where grass grows. "We're very proud to see how clean the creek remains after a rain," says Greg. "Things farmers have learned over the last twenty years have contributed to a healthier environment."

In 2001, Greg, along with sons Chris and Tyler and daughter Jessica, decided to produce their own wine. Chris is the winemaker. Tyler coordinates special projects such as getting part of the ranch organically certified and complying with Fish Friendly Farming practices. They and their families, and Greg and his wife Missy, all live on the ranch.

The first Nelson wine was Pinot Grigio because it was an up-and-comer, says Greg. The family sat down together and tasted sixteen flights of Pinot Grigio to figure out what style they liked. "No one spit during the entire tasting," laughs Greg. They settled on an Italian style that is clean and crisp.

"For a consumer who is meticulous about wine, a small winery like ours has such a hands-on approach, you can taste it in the glass," says Greg. Nelson wines include Pinot Grigio, Riesling, Viognier, Chardonnay, Cabernet Sauvignon and Zinfandel, as well as a fruity, sweet Orange Muscat. They also have their olives crushed and sell the oil in the tasting room.

With a ranch filled with thriving enterprises, Nelson Family Vineyards blends the old with the contemporary. Each generation infused new energy into this beautiful ranch north of Hopland, building upon tradition always a step ahead of the times.

ALL IN THE FAMILY

Most of Mendocino's wineries and vineyards are family-owned. As often as not, you'll find the owners on hand when you stop by a tasting room. Multi-generations still live on former pear, apple and sheep ranches throughout the county with their children or grandkids playing in the vineyards and gardens. In some families, the younger set left for college and returned, with a renewed interest in the family business. Others moved back to Mendocino County later, when it was time to raise a family. Of the wineries profiled in this book, nearly all are family-owned. The following is only a sampling of the family theme that is repeated throughout this collection of stories.

HUSCH VINEYARDS
HOME SWEET HUSCH

FOURSIGHT
LOGGERS TO VINTNERS

MEYER FAMILY CELLARS
RAISING KIDS AND GRAPES

BELLS ECHO
SUTTON FAMILY'S BIG ADVENTURE

PETTRONE
A FAMILY BRAND

HUSCH VINEYARDS

HOME SWEET HUSCH

"I love hearing people say Husch hasn't changed!" says Amanda Robinson Holstine, a mother of two and one of the family owners at Husch Vineyards. She and her brother Zac Robinson, along with their parents and spouses, are at the Husch helm today.

Their grandfather, Hugo Oswald, didn't start Husch, the oldest winery in Anderson Valley. That honor belongs to namesakes Tony and Gretchen Husch, who planted the vineyard in 1968 and established the winery in 1971. When Tony Husch put the winery up for sale eight years later, Oswald walked the vineyard with him and they sealed the deal.

"Grand Oz, our grandfather's nickname, grew grapes and he wanted to make wine for the locals—something everyone can afford," Amanda recounts. Hugh Oswald and his wife Bea lived at La Ribera Ranch on Old River Road south of Ukiah. They were second and third generation Mendocino farmers and had seven children, including the Robinsons' mother, Beelu. When Beelu married Richard Robinson they became the next generation to continue the Husch winery.

"Our parents would bring us with them when they came over to work in the salesroom on the weekends," says Zac, vice president of operations. As kids, they tromped around the vineyard and splashed in the creek, just like their children now do. A seven-story treehouse built in the grove of redwood trees was added on to by each generation.

Colorful heritage roses climb the rough-hewn redwood siding of the tasting room, formerly one of the original homesteader dwellings. "Instead of the cashbox our parents used, we have a computerized cash register now," said Amanda, with a laugh.

Located about ten miles northwest of Boonville, the understated entrance is bordered by a row of redwood trees along Highway 128. The Robinsons and their families live in Ukiah but are at the winery regularly, often with their spouses and offspring.

Amanda's husband Brad Holstine, is Husch's winemaker. He continues the tradition of making Husch's Big Six—Sauvignon Blanc, Chardonnay, Cabernet Sauvignon, Pinot Noir, Chenin Blanc and Gewurztraminer. He loves it when people come up at wine tastings and tell him, "I recognize this wine." He also employs his talents creating small wine lots like Renegade Sauvignon Blanc, aged in neutral oak with wild yeast, LA Blanc, a fresh white wine, and MoJo Red, named for the current generation's children.

The Husch experience continues from the tasting room to the self-guided vineyard tour. You can't go in the winter when the neighboring sheep are grazing among the vines. Otherwise, ask the tasting room staff for the printed guide. The walk takes as little as fifteen minutes or as long as you like to mosey among the vines, checking out the seven points of interest. You'll learn a bit of Husch history as well as a few things about grape growing at this certified Fish Friendly vineyard.

The tour begins near an owl box, one of four around the sixty-acre property, wends through the vineyard rows into the redwood grove and up to a knoll. From the top you can see classic Anderson Valley views of oak trees, redwoods and the sloped hillsides that surround the old craftsman-style homestead.

There's no place like Husch.

FOURSIGHT WINERY
LOGGERS TO VINTNERS

Past and present mix with ease at the Foursight vineyards, where four generations of the Charles family have made their living in the middle of Boonville since the 1940s. From logging to grape-growing, each has built upon their love and respect for their family land.

The thirty-two-acre family farm between Highway 128 and Anderson Creek was once the site of Charles Lumber Company, founded by the father and grandfather of the current patriarch, Bill Charles. Chickens, a vege table garden and an organic hay field have been part of the scene since the 1950s, when Bill was growing up here. At that time, worker housing surrounded the mill. "I waited with as many as thirty other children at the end of the driveway for the school bus," he recalls.

Bill and his wife Nancy live in the house where Bill was born. Their daughter Kristy and her husband Joe Webb, Foursight's winemaker, live in the house where Kristy and her two brothers were raised.

Bill built the redwood-sided tasting room with wood from the property. "We dug up old trees and milled them," he says. Some of the logs were buried on the property for fifty years.

In 2001 the Charles family planted fifteen acres of their favorite varietals, Pinot Noir and Sauvignon Blanc. Behind the winery, an orchard of mature walnut, quince, loquat, apple, wild plum and fig trees shade a picnic space.

The grapes grown at the Charles' ranch are the product of "a lot of tedious manual labor," says Nancy, who considers the 3,163 vines her babies. Bill can be seen on his tractor in the vineyard, his notebook in hand, jotting down which vine needs more compost or which one looks especially vigorous. "Can't farm vineyards by neglect," he says.

Foursight's name is a play on words that honor four generations with vision. As Kristy points out, although she and Webb are millennials, and their parents are baby boomers, their attachment to the ranch helps the family to continue making a living on her grandparents' land.

MEYER FAMILY CELLARS

RAISING KIDS AND GRAPES

Around one of the bends on Highway 128, halfway from Boonville to Yorkville, is Meyer Family Cellars, a refreshing wayside stop — especially if you're traveling with kids who need to get out of the car and play!

The Meyers' winery is not only a destination. It is where Matt and Karen Meyer live with their two daughters. The driveway is lined with blooming plants, many of them natives. A trellis-covered picnic area with the pint-sized redwood gym sits next to a vineyard. The cool tasting room with rust-colored walls and a smooth handcrafted bar is the place to taste Meyer Family Cellars wines.

Matt is the son of Bonnie and the late Justin Meyer, co-founders of the esteemed Silver Oak Cellars in Napa Valley. Karen is the daughter of wine shop proprietors in Perth, Australia. After growing up in separate hemispheres, Karen and Matt's paths converged.

"I grew up working in vineyards," says Matt. He and his two siblings were raised near Oakville in Napa Valley. Through his teens, he spent summers working in the vineyard, tasting room and cellar at Silver Oak. He went to Washington to college and finished at Lewis and Clark. Although he spent some time in Australia, Matt didn't meet Karen until they were both working the harvest at a winery in Oregon. They moved to California and married in 2006.

"My parents' wine shop exposed me to nice wines at a young age," says Karen. Her first job was working in a winery. She then earned an enology degree at Charles Sturt University in New South Wales. It is common for budding Aussie winemakers to cross to the Northern Hemisphere "racking up harvests in the US and Europe."

When Matt's parents sold Silver Oak, they began making Zinfandel Port and were looking for a place to produce it when they found and purchased this acreage. The family built the beautiful redwood winery in 1993.

The Meyers make 1,000 cases of Port. "There are different ways to get to Port," explains Matt. He makes their Port from old vine Zinfandel grapes grown in Mendocino County. It is fortified with brandy from Mendocino County's Jaxon Keys or Germain-Robin distilleries. "By the time it's in the tasting room," says Matt, "our Port is an average of eight to nine years old." He explains that it takes time for the fruit flavors and alcohol to settle down and bond into a jammy, smooth mouthful, which gets better with age. The alcohol in Meyer's Port is around eighteen percent.

In addition to Port, Syrah is the passion of these young winemakers. Syrah also happens to be a popular varietal in Australia where it is known as Shiraz. For rosé lovers, Meyer's Rosé of Syrah is a must try.

Matt likes the climate of their property in Yorkville Highlands. "Syrah has a tendency to shrivel and cook if the grapes get too hot and can't cool down," says Matt. The days get hot but not as hot as in Cloverdale, thirty miles away. Even though Meyer Family Cellars is around fifty miles from the ocean, the coastal influence is felt daily when the wind kicks up and cools everything down for the night. "It's fifteen degrees cooler here at night than in Cloverdale," he adds.

Matt is the "vineyard guy" and Karen is the winemaker, "but we don't have titles," says Karen. "We both do everything." That includes hosting the popular Yorkville Highlands Festival in August each year. As for their kids, they love to play with the children who visit when their parents stop at the tasting room. Grownups will find the bocce court and horseshoe pit pretty fun for their own respite from the winding road.

BELLS ECHO
SUTTON FAMILY'S BIG ADVENTURE

Like the homesteading Italians in the 1880s, and the back-to-the-landers of the 1970s, Lisa and Ron Sutton were drawn by the beauty of Mendocino County, the fresh air, acres to hike and bike and making a living from the land. Unlike their earlier counterparts, the Suttons were in search of a weekend place to spend quality time with their twins Sam and Alessandra.

"We weren't looking for a vineyard," says Lisa, who grew up in Southern California. "I'd never been farther north than Healdsburg."

Ron grew up next to Lake Minnewaska in Minnesota. His parents had a hobby farm with cattle and horses and the rural setting was "a Garrison Keillor town" with ice fishing, farming and a resort.

Within a few years of getting married and having twins, the handsome architect and the beautiful physical therapist became grape growers. Their home sits on a terraced knoll overlooking fifty acres of vines off Feliz Creek Road west of Hopland.

"From the moment we saw this place, the wheels started and kept turning in this direction," says Ron, as his blue eyes light up from beneath his wide-brimmed cowboy hat. "I became interested in investing in something long-term for the family," adds Lisa.

"What a place to spend time with the kids," she says. "I thought if they can grow up here it would be extraordinary. There are rocks to climb, streams to wade, a pond to skinny dip and it is so gorgeous." While they knew it would be challenging, it seemed that the vineyards were a bonus and could help pay for the place. They couldn't quit their day jobs and they knew nothing about growing or selling grapes, but they plunged ahead.

In 2005, the Suttons bought the ranch, once part of the Sanel Valley Rancho, an old Mexican land grant. The Suttons improved the ranch's sustainable growing practices as they move toward organic farming. Their ten acres of Merlot and five of Petite Verdot became California Certified Organic in 2010. "We keep the crop loads down and use little water," says Ron, adding, "It's true, you need good grapes to make great wine."

The Suttons grow red Bordeaux varietals including Cabernet Sauvignon, Merlot, Petite Verdot, Malbec and Syrah. Ron does the marketing with print pieces, the website and a vineyard newsletter.

While their main focus is growing "unique, intriguing fruit," Ron says, "We delight in seeing and tasting this fruit being made into equally exciting wines. We enjoy the experience of working closely with the winemaker; from pruning and watering, to shoot, leaf and cluster management- all the way to harvest."

Adding to the prestigious list of wines made from Bells Echo grapes, the Suttons stepped into winemaking on a small scale. They produce Boar Block Merlot, named for the herd of pigs some hunter friends rounded up with their "pig posse" and Buckeye Rock Cabernet Sauvignon, named for the giant rock that sports a buckeye tree growing from it. Add Bells Echo Honeybee Malbec, Serendipity Syrah and Cinnabear Syrah and check the website for availability and other clever monikers.

"We have fallen so in love with this—the seasons, the beauty of the cover crops in the spring and walking or running through the vineyards with Sam and Alessandra," says Lisa, who drives the tractor at harvest. She adds, "What we get to do here as a family is so rewarding."

PETTRONE
A FAMILY BRAND

Bound by their love of Italy, France's Rhône Valley and their lives in Mendocino County, Kati Pettrone and Skip Bailey Lovin became partners with Pettrone's brothers, Mark and Frank, to establish Pettrone Family Cellars.

The garage winery, which is not open to the public, is nestled against the western hills of Ukiah Valley. The setting, around a beautifully restored and decorated farmhouse, includes all the elements of an idyllic Mediterranean rural lifestyle. The driveway is bordered with a line of Italian cypress trees and a hedgerow of lavender. Three acres of Syrah and Grenache, varietals from Skip's favorite wine region in France—the southern Rhône—are terraced facing south and east to catch the early and midday sun.

Kati's vegetable garden proliferates from summer through fall in lettuces, onions, chard, tomatoes, squash and peppers. Thirty olive trees, planted in 2002, are her passion. Their olives join the harvests of other local hobby olive growers, to be pressed into oil and bottled for their use until the next year's crop is in.

Kati was born in New York, where her brothers still live. Their late mother, Pia, was six months old when she emigrated with her family from Val di Rendena in northern Italy. Their father, the late Angelo Pettrone, came with his family from Sicily. Angelo became an attorney and commuted to Manhattan every day from Fayetteville, New York, where he and Pia raised their three children.

In 1981, Kati was studying at the University of California, Berkeley, when she joined the back-to-the-land movement, following some friends to Potter Valley in eastern Mendocino County where they built a geodesic dome. She moved in with her children, Chandra and Nate Gilmore.

Skip, born in San Francisco, spent his early years in Texas, where his medical doctor dad was in the Army Air Corps, and then with the University of Texas in Galveston. He and his family moved to the Los Angeles area "one year before Disneyland opened and the Dodgers moved there." He says, "It couldn't have been a better place for a kid to grow up."

He went on to UC Davis. "I liked Science and Organic Chemistry," he explains, and got a degree in food science. In 1972, around the same time he finished college, his father and brother bought a cattle ranch in Potter Valley. They decided to switch to grape growing and Skip was invited to manage the property.

In between clearing land and planting one hundred acres of Riesling and Pinot Noir grapes,

"I made my own wine," says Skip. After his father passed away, and with the arrival of phylloxera, the family sold the vineyard. Over the years, Skip managed other vineyards and now works as a grower relations representative for a large winery in Sonoma County.

Kati and Skip met in 1987 when both were living in Potter Valley. For the next decade the two traveled occasionally to France and Italy visiting wineries, Kati practicing her French and Italian and Skip collecting wine. In 1998, they purchased and moved to their property south of Ukiah, where they built a wine cellar adjacent to their bonded winery. Skip has about 2000 bottles of wine in his cellar, three-quarters of them from Europe and a third from southern France's Rhône region.

When Skip and Kati and her brothers decided to make wine to honor the Pettrone Italian heritage they designed their wine label to do just that. It has Tuscan terra cotta colored lines on cream paper, three birds and a tiny block encapsulating "AP3." AP3 stands for Angelo Pettrone and his three offspring, who are also represented as the three birds in the crest. Pettrone Family Cellars' Mendocino-style Chianti is made from Sangiovese, the main grape in Italy's renowned Chianti.

"It was customary to have wine at the table when my brothers and I were growing up," says Kati. "Our Pettrone Sangiovese reminds us of the wine of our childhood."

GROWING A SENSE OF PLACE

Whether their family was born in Mendocino County or came from elsewhere, vintners from Mendocino are noteworthy for their fierce protection of the land and their commitment to preserving and honoring what nature provides. It shows in their vineyard, their wines and their approach to life. All of the vineyards and wineries in this book could be in this section; these are profiled for their unique approaches and styles.

WEIBEL FAMILY WINERY
FULL CIRCLE

LAZY CREEK
IDYLLIC SETTING AND SIZE

JAXON KEYS
WINERY AND DISTILLERY

RIVINO
A NATURAL PROGRESSION

CAMPOVIDA
GARDEN AND WINE DESTINATION

Weibel Family Winery

Full Circle

Before coming to Mendocino in the 1970s, Weibel was one of California's big family-owned wineries. Long before establishing themselves here, the family patriarch Rudolf Weibel made wine in his native Switzerland.

In the 1930s, after immigrating to the United States, Rudolf and his son Fred Sr. garnered quite a reputation trucking in grapes and making sparkling wine in the basement of the William Tell Hotel in San Francisco.

In 1946, looking to expand, the Weibels heard about and purchased a one hundred-acre historic ranch with vineyards and dilapidated winery in what was then known as Mission San Jose, now Fremont. It had originally belonged to Governor Leland Stanford, who was selling it to put resources into what was to become Stanford University on another farm up the peninsula.

By the mid-1950s, Weibel Winery was known not only for sparkling wine, but also for their Green Hungarian wine. The slightly sweet white wine was beloved by many of a generation that was just discovering wine after World War II.

Two decades later, in 1971, the Weibels expanded north to Mendocino County. They built a tasting room and winery along Highway 101 in Redwood Valley north of Ukiah. The design of the tasting room was modeled after an inverted champagne glass in honor of the popular sparkling wine Weibel continues to produce. In 1995, the tasting room was purchased by Charlie and Martha Barra and continues as Barra of Mendocino.

The Weibel family kept other vineyards in Mendocino County. After fifty years of being headquartered in San Jose, third generation owner, Fred Weibel, Jr. and his wife Judy, relocated the winery to Woodbridge near Lodi in central California. Their son Justin is part of the team as a winemaker.

In 2006, the family returned to Mendocino County. Their tasting room joins three other Mendocino tasting rooms on the east side of downtown Hopland.

The Weibels still make their popular California champagnes and four fruit-flavored sparkling wines called Sparkelle. All Weibel sparkling wine begins with French Colombard grapes. After fermentation, the wine becomes bubbly by the charmant method whereby a cold secondary fermentation takes place in stainless steel tanks. Their Grand Cuvée is an off-dry sparkler with small bubbles and go-with-everything flavor. Their Stanford Brut "has elements of peach, apricot and hazelnut."

All the Sparkelle flavors come from natural ingredients and include pomegranate, peach, raspberry and almond. Tasting room manager Margaret Pedroni invented a Mendocino cocktail made with Raspberry Sparkelle, raspberry vodka, Triple Sec and Chambord.

In addition, Weibel produces other labels honoring Mendocino wine connections. Their Road I label designates white and red table wines made from Mendocino County grapes grown on their vineyards. The white is a blend of Sauvignon Blanc and Chardonnay and the red combines Merlot and Syrah.

Their Truscott label honors Samuel Z. Truscott, a pioneer in the California wine industry. As legend has it, Truscott did everything from distribute the wines made in San Francisco basements to work harvest, crush and make wine alongside the immigrant Italian and Swiss vintners in Sonoma County. He ultimately settled in Mendocino County with his family and planted a vineyard.

The Weibel winery tradition has come full circle to continue their presence in Mendocino County. Their focus is on Weibel family classics including Sauvignon Blanc, Chardonnay, Pinot Noir and Zinfandel. Much of the fruit comes from Weibel family vineyards in Redwood Valley and Potter Valley.

Lazy Creek
Idyllic Setting and Size

For many who become Lazy Creek aficionados, tasting Lazy Creek wine at a restaurant or on a friend's recommendation often precedes a visit. One drive up the meandering shady lane lined by weathered split rail fencing, however, and the charming setting not only infatuates, but the total experience seals the deal. This is the winery everyone wishes was theirs.

Falling in love with Lazy Creek is as easy as driving through the front gate, say owners Don and Rhonda Carano, proprietors of Ferrari-Carano Winery in Sonoma County.

Lazy Creek was established in 1973 by Theresia and the late Hans Kobler, who had been a longtime waiter at the legendary Jack's and Blue Fox restaurants in San

Francisco. When the Koblers discovered Anderson Valley, this was the old Pinoli homestead and plum trees were the crop. Hans planted Gewurztraminer, Chardonnay and Pinot Noir vines that he brought from Europe by suitcase to connect his Old World heritage with his Anderson Valley abode.

Before long other new vintners followed suit, and Gewurztraminer and Pinot Noir put Anderson Valley on America's winegrowing map. These wines are showcased at the annual Anderson Valley Pinot Noir and International Alsatian Varietals Festivals.

The Koblers converted the Pinoli's old barn to a winery. They stacked barrels by hand on top of each other pyramid style and offered tastings at the picnic table by the ramshackle farmhouse. Today, the barrels are on racks and the tasting room evokes a compelling blend of old and contemporary.

The ranch has been sustainably farmed for forty years. Lazy Creek's heritage Pinot Noir, Chardonnay and Gewurztraminer vineyards continue to be the winery focus. Since the Caranos purchased in 2008, they have continued to maintain the vineyards and have planted more varietals. All the grapes for Lazy Creek wines are grown on the property. In addition to well-rounded, luscious Pinot Noir, no-oak Chablis-style Chardonnay and classic dry Gewurztraminer, Lazy Creek wines now include Riesling, Syrah and Pinot Noir Rosé.

Lazy Creek is situated in a small bowl at the end of the tree-lined drive just off Highway 128 in Anderson Valley. Next to the parking lot a weathered redwood tractor shed is surrounded by rolling vineyards. A 1940s flatbed pickup is parked where it's been for decades. Barrels are stacked on the bed and a painting of it hangs in the tasting room.

Rusty red corrugated siding antiquates the exterior of the tasting room but inside, contemporary lines and colors frame large plate-glass doors and picture windows. The tasting room attracts locals who bring visiting friends, as well as fans who have followed Lazy Creek for years. Handcrafted barn wood serves as the tasting bar and the broad, high windows flood the room with light from the south, west and north. The wine is packaged in high quality glass with heavy rims and elegant wax-like caps. Each bottle is numbered and the label captures the winery scene in a pewter-colored line drawing.

Taking in the intimate landscape with the loyal following, it's normal to find other Lazy Creek fans at the winery who proudly say,

"I love it here."

WINERY AND DISTILLERY

The eye-catching farmhouse with the inviting wraparound porch perch on a knoll next to Highway 101 north of Hopland, Jaxon Keys is the only winery in the United States to also have a distillery. The 1,250-acre ranch was once part of the northernmost Mexican land grant, awarded in the 1800s to John McGlashen. He was a Scottish immigrant who named the estate "Burnee Hill Ranch" meaning "house on a hill."

The owners of the beautiful ranch that spans both sides of Highway 101 are Ken and Diane Wilson. The Wilsons began as vineyard owners in Sonoma County who realized their dream of producing estate-grown wines when they started Wilson Winery in 1993. They have subsequently purchased other high-end artisan wineries with estate vineyards. They named Jaxon Keys after their respective grandparents, Jack Wilson and Cecil Keys.

Their winemaker, Fred Nickel, is a veteran Mendocino vintner, whose career parallels the growth of the Mendocino wine industry. While at UC Davis Fred majored in viticulture, but decided winemaking was a lot more fun than grape growing.

In 1979, he arrived in Mendocino County and worked in the cellar during harvest with the late Barney Fetzer and Paul Dolan at Fetzer Vineyards when it was still in Redwood Valley.

Through the 1980s, when wineries were sprouting up in Mendocino and Lake Counties, Fred worked with some of the best. In addition to the Fetzers, he had a stint with Mendocino's wine patriarch John Parducci. He was the first winemaker for the late Jess Jackson (when he was in Lake County), spent time at Tijsseling Winery in McNab Valley, which is now McNab Ridge, and was the winemaker at Brutocao Cellars in Hopland.

Fred started at Jaxon Keys in 2010. In addition to Sauvignon Blanc, which has an affinity for this ranch's terroir and has always been a local favorite, Fred makes Jaxon Keys estate-grown Chardonnay, Syrah, Petite Sirah, Cabernet Sauvignon and Zinfandel.

In the old French alembic copper still, housed next to the winery, Fred guides wine made from fifty-year-old Colombard vines as it is distilled into cognac-quality brandy. The brandy is bottled under the Jepson label, which pays tribute to the previous owner who began growing grapes and making wine and brandy on this property in the 1980s.

Fred's philosophy reflects the owners' estate-grown mission for their wine portfolio. "During harvest, I'm cognizant of what each varietal is doing in every block of vines," he says. "My goal is to bring the vines up to reach their true potential, then step back and let the wine do its thing."

In addition to its beautifully remodeled tasting room and appealing panoramic view from the surrounding veranda, Jaxon Keys offers a guesthouse to rent... and prolong the stay on this historic ranch.

RIVINO
A NATURAL PROGRESSION

A serendipitous meeting in Mendocino County brought former residents of Vancouver, British Columbia, Suzanne Jahnke-McConnell and Jason McConnell together. Their winery, RIVINO, located just off Highway 101 south of Ukiah at Schrader Ranch Vineyard, was established in 2007.

Born in London, Suzanne grew up in Vancouver, moved to Houston, Texas, and then went into the family's property-management business. After Suzanne's father, Gordon Jahnke, bought the Schrader Ranch in the early 1990s, Suzanne got involved with the vineyards.

Jason, who has a mechanical engineering degree, started making home wine as a hobby when he was still in Vancouver. He was transferring to Ukiah for a job when he and Suzanne met.

In the summer of 2003, Suzanne and Jason were standing in line to attend the John Ash cooking class at a Mendocino wine event in Hopland. They started talking and discovered they were both from Canada and had graduated from the University of British Columbia. "I invited him to sit at our table for dinner during the auction and that was that," says Suzanne.

They both love wine. Suzanne was drawn to winemaking because grapes surrounded her. "When I came here in 1998, my dad sold all our grapes. I was curious to find out what our grapes could do," she says. As the fall harvest began, she and Jason decided to make a little Chardonnay and Merlot under the barn and "it turned out quite nice." They married that December in British Columbia.

"We are a small operation," says Jason. "At harvest, the tractor pulls up with the bins and within a couple of hours of picking, we are working on the grapes." While Jason does the bulk of the winemaking chores from crush to bottling, together they work on the final tasting, blends and sales. "It's very hands-on here," says Suzanne.

They love having the luxury of choosing the blocks of vines from the two hundred acres on the ranch. Jason describes a favorite Cabernet Franc block on top of a knoll. "We also like the middle section of the Merlot block between a giant oak tree and the river," he says. "And the Chardonnay on the river is great. It grows these tall vines, that we can actually walk underneath."

The Russian River inspired RIVINO's name. "It's our combination of Russian River and vino," explains Suzanne. RIVINO also means "river" in Italian. Artist Cameron Bird did the oil painting of the river on the label.

"I don't know if it's our proximity to the Russian River, but I know the nutrients in the soil help make our grapes prize winners," says Jason. RIVINO's first Viognier and Chardonnay won gold medals at the 2009 Mendocino County Fair Wine competition.

Wine tastings at RIVINO always include something to eat and suggestions on what to serve with the wines. At times, Jason serves what he calls "wine snaps" which are paper-thin cracker-like wafers he makes with raisins, pecans, flax, pumpkin seed and a hint of rosemary. When the Sangiovese grapes ripen to the point of raisins, he substitutes the raisiny grapes for commercial raisins.

"We give visitors a tour to the depth of their hearts' desires," says Jason. He will explain "as much of the nitty-gritty about the wine making process as they want." When Suzanne and Jason have time to get away, the couple most often head off on a wine sales trip. They live close to the Ukiah airport, a good thing since both are pilots and love to fly.

CAMPOVIDA

GARDEN AND WINE DESTINATION

The epitome of the best of Mendocino style is concentrated on a few acres just east of Hopland at Campovida. Lush organic gardens, trellised archways covered with edible vines, a high stone wall encircling a Tuscan garden, beehives, olive trees, a pond-side pavilion with demonstration kitchen and fruit orchards encompass a serene setting with entertaining and event spaces. The avant-garde tasting room and the tastefully appointed lodging allow immersion into this "field of life" that translates to Campovida.

From the moment in 2010, when they first set foot on what was formerly known as Valley Oaks ranch, Anna Beuselinck and Gary Breen were inspired by the opportunity to integrate their work and living with historic and familial connections on this fully organic ranch.

Valley Oaks, now Campovida, was part of an 1844 Mexican land grant to cattle rancher Fernando Feliz. Over the years, the fertile bottomland acreage changed hands to other farmers, who raised animals and crops, including hops. The barns and big house were constructed in the 1890s.

Mendocino's renowned wine family, the Fetzers, purchased Valley Oaks in 1984, remodeling the facility to become one of Wine Country's premier entertainment and event facilities. Gary and Anna are revitalizing that reputation.

"We had a dream to live in the country," say Anna and Gary, who both grew up in suburban Bay Area communities. Living in Oakland at the time and having two small daughters, they were drawn to a new and compelling commitment to what they are calling "integrated living."

"I don't think of this as ours—we are spending our little bit of time here like families before us. We appreciate the land and what it gives as did the native Pomos for 10,000 years before we got here," says Anna.

Taking responsibility as stewards of the property, Gary and Anna revitalized the gardens and put a fresh face on the historic barns, the pavilion and "bones" that make this a wine, food, community and family experience.

"This is the coolest thing we could ever do," says Gary, whose business in the Bay Area included refurbishing derelict lots into unimaginable charm. "He is a developer of possibilities," says Anna. "She's a developer of leaders," says Gary. Anna is an executive coach focusing on global thought leadership.

First stop is the tasting room where delving into the history and the philosophy of Campovida begins. Gary is often found greeting tasters at the copper-topped circular bar. Historic artwork, framed in barnwood, and seasonal photographs of the property are on the walls. Campovida wine is made from grapes grown on the ranch, including the Viogner vineyard you pass coming in along the elm tree lined drive. Mendocino Farms wines are made from special vineyards around Mendocino. "We want our wine to tell the stories of those who grow grapes in Mendocino," says Gary. Campovida also offers estate-grown honey and olive oil.

You can take a glass of wine and stroll the property to get the full experience. The refurbished lodging is painted a spring green and the eco-friendly swimming pool is filled with saltwater to avoid chlorination. Surrounding palm trees are cleaned to keep them from incessantly dropping fronds. A border of flowering tobacco blazes a white and purple haze next to the old barn, now an events facility.

Into the garden, nourished by master gardener Ken Boek, you pass through the hummingbird and wedding gardens. Voices of other visitors hum through the foliage, the multi-bloomed Sally Holmes roses, Matilija poppies and the anise hys-sop. Lettuce, herbs and more vegetables flourish in luxuriant rows. In the gazebo-trellised Tuscan garden, handcrafted benches invite a moment for meditation and immersion in the natural beauty.

Campovida is a quintessential Mendocino destination and an extraordinary event facility for weddings, corporate retreats and special occasion events.

Settled onto this historic land, Gary and Anna are realizing their dream to live, work and raise their children at Campovida. As resident proprietors they breathe and appreciate the amenities around them. As inveterate hosts they are pleased to share their experience in this unique setting. "Mother Nature is such a humbling boss," says Anna.

Close to the rugged, sparsely populated Mendocino coast dotted with historic towns, the cool climate and summer fog contribute to the quality of certain grape varietals. Riesling, Pinot Noir, Syrah and Zinfandel thrive within sight of the Pacific Ocean near Elk and Point Arena on the south Mendocino Coast. The Mendocino Ridge American Viticultural Area (AVA), America's only non-contiguous AVA, skims coastal mountaintops parallel to the Pacific. In addition to Drew and Mariah, other vineyards within sight of the ocean include Manchester Ridge, Ferrari-Carano's Sky High, Valenti, Perli, Wiley and Greenwood Ridge. One winery, Pacific Star, crushes inland-grown grapes on a bluff off Highway 1, crediting the quality of its wine to the winery's isolation and proximity to the sea air. Other prominent labels that use grapes grown within range of the ocean include Greg La Follette, Black Kite, Philips Hill and Baxter.

PACIFIC STAR
LOCATION TO A FAULT

MARIAH VINEYARDS
ISLANDS IN THE SKY

DREW FAMILY CELLARS
RIDGE TO THE SEA

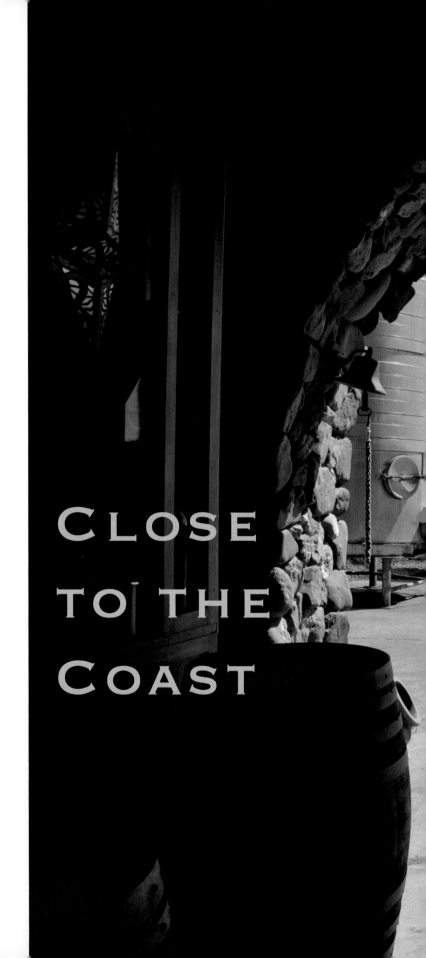

CLOSE TO THE COAST

PACIFIC STAR
LOCATION TO A FAULT

Pacific Star is the only winery in California perched on bluffs above the ocean. Twelve miles north of Fort Bragg, the magnificent location of winemaker Sally's Ottoson's business and home on the Mendocino Coast is worth the trip. Besides its proximity to lapping waves, passing whales, amazing sunsets and variety of signature-blend wines poured daily, there's another item of interest at Pacific Star.

A recently discovered earthquake fault line transverses surf and cliff underneath the stone-and-redwood winery. Appropriately named in 2006, the Pacific Star Fault connects eventually to the more famous San Andreas Fault. It's a strike-slip fault moving laterally and horizontally at the same time says Ottoson. Sally named a multiple vintage Syrah, Charbono and Carignane "It's My Fault." She recommends this as the perfect wine to "keep under the bed when you want to say I'm sorry."

Pacific Star's founder and winemaker doggedly pursues her craft in the Scandinavian spirit she was born with. Tall, with striking good looks, Sally loves to fish as much as she loves to make wine.

Born and raised in Fort Bragg, she spent twenty years in the Napa Valley wine country before coming back to the Mendocino coast. In addition to her winery just south of the tiny village of Westport, a place she came as a kid to fish with her family, she opened a tasting room in downtown Fort Bragg.

In 1861, Sally's grandfather came to Comptche with the Oppenlanders and homesteaded in what is now known as Surprise Valley. "Growing up, Dad took me hunting and fishing, and we all made jams and pickles and canned albacore," she says.

In 1988, on a visit home to see her parents in Fort Bragg, Sally decided she was ready to come back to the coast. When a realtor showed her the fifteen-acre parcel just south of Westport, Sally envisioned its possibilities.

Over the past twenty years, she built the stone-and-redwood winery and her home above it. She started sourcing her grapes in Mendocino County when she bought Charbono from Eddie Graziano's vineyard in Calpella. "Charbono is the basis of my business," she says. This Old World grape planted by the Italian settlers was once one of California's most popular blending grapes. It had almost lost its popularity when Sally discovered it.

Charbono, she says, "represents everything I like about wine. It's not high in acid or tannin. It's not pretentious. It's a sit-down-and-drink-me wine."

And she likes it because there are no preconceived notions about it. "Most people don't know what Charbono 'should' taste like and it goes with just about everything."

Sally makes about fifteen wines. Pacific Star's red varietals include Pinot Noir, Merlot, Barbera, Zinfandel and Petite Sirah, in addition to Charbono. Red signature blends include a one-of-a-kind Charbera, made from half Charbono and half Barbera.

All Pacific Star wine is made at the cliffside winery framed in stone and cooled by the natural climate. Outside, picnic tables and Adirondack chairs perch along the bluffs for gazing at the ocean.

Inside the tasting room, a handcrafted polished slab of redwood straddles wine barrels and serves as a bar. There is an eye-catching swirl of color on the floor, painted by Robert Minuzzo, an artist from Napa. He spent a month dumping and swirling paint on the floor to replicate his vision of the faultline, which runs under the building.

Sally says she often looked over the edge of the cliffs and noticed some erosion and deep caves and patterns, which now she knows occurs because of the fault line. She says, "When the fault was discovered, it confirmed my feeling that there was something extremely unique about this place." The drive along Highway One is worth it.

MARIAH VINEYARDS

ISLANDS IN THE SKY

Mariah Vineyards is off the grid, powered by solar energy, a biodiesel generator and tractors. At 2,400-foot elevation and with views of the Pacific Ocean, Mariah is one of the few vineyards within the only noncontiguous American Viticulture Area (AVA) in America. It is officially called Mendocino Ridge, but Mariah's proprietors refer to the appellation as "islands in the sky."

For Dan and Vicki Dooling, two native San Franciscans, to find their way to this Mendocino wilderness, the path included a childhood prophecy, a lot of miles trucking, and a dream. Dan's mother's Italian family had a vineyard in Santa Rosa. Dan grew up visiting it, but the idea of having his own vineyard was seeded by a close friend of Dan's father named Ed Bernard. Ed moved from San Francisco to Napa Valley in the 1950s and planted grapes on his 2,000 acres near the Veterans Home in Yountville.

One weekend, in the early 1960s, when Dan was eleven years old, he noticed a line of little flags in Ed's vineyard and asked about them. "Ed put his arm on my shoulders looking at those flags and said, 'Dan, someday you will have a vineyard where there will be no reason to put a freeway through it.'" Highway 29 was constructed right through Ed's property.

When Dan and Vicky met in San Francisco in the early 1970s, the two were drawn to the wine country and Dan got work putting in vineyards in Napa Valley. He was making $3.10 an hour laboring in the vineyards when his dad, who drove truck for a supermarket chain for forty years, called him. "Dad said I could make fifty grand driving a truck for Hamm's Brewery," he remembers. Dan headed back to the city and went to work driving truck so he could save up to buy land.

Between 1973 and 1978, he and Vicki spent every weekend looking for vineyard property. "On New Year's Day in 1978, we looked at this land in Mendocino County. It was snowing!"

Within a year they bought ninety-one acres. It was forested, but had south-facing slopes, gentle to rolling to nearly flat. "This property has the best black loam soil," says Dooling. In 1980, Dan planted their first twenty acres of Zinfandel vines. They later added Syrah and Pinot Noir.

Mariah Vineyards' first commercial crop of grapes was sold to winemaker Jed Steele in 1983. In the Dooling's small winery underneath their home, they produce about 650 cases of prized Zinfandel and Syrah.

In 1997, Dan and Steve Alden, who also has a Mendocino ridgetop vineyard on nearby Fish Rock Road, spearheaded the formation of America's only noncontiguous AVA. An American Viticultural Area identifies the unique and shared geographic, climate and soil characteristics of a specific wine-growing region.

One of the most identifiable features of these "islands in the sky" above the fog line is the intensity of light at the Mendocino Ridge elevations, which range from 1,200 feet to Mariah's 2,400 feet. The growing season lasts from April through November, and the Doolings have seen temperatures vary "up to 105 degrees and down to 17 degrees" over the years. Winter snow powders the vineyard occasionally. An AVA has to be named for historical or geographic references. While the ridges that form Mendocino Ridge AVA appear like islands floating in the summer fog or winter clouds, they couldn't get it named "Islands in the Sky." Vicky and Dan have since trademarked the name.

It took three and a half years to get approval for the Mendocino Ridge AVA. Mendocino Ridge appellation includes vineyards that were planted in the 1850s such as Zeni and Ciapusci on Fish Rock Road. There are a dozen vineyards and five wineries in the Mendocino Ridge AVA, including Mariah, Drew, Greenwood Ridge, Baxter, and Mendocino Ridge.

The Mariah wine label features a drawing of a woman with pale green grape-leaf hair blowing on a cream-colored background.

DREW FAMILY CELLARS
RIDGE TO THE SEA

On a clear day you can see the ocean from the deck of Molly and Jason Drew's home above the barn-styled winery. Molly and Jason are raising their two sons on this former apple ranch three miles from the Pacific Ocean on Greenwood Ridge.

They are among the most recent generation of young winemakers to buy into a rural lifestyle that comes with raising grapes and children in Mendocino County. Molly and Jason purchased twenty-six acres from Stuart Beck, who produces Greenwood Gold Apple Juice.

"Part of the charm of the ranch is the apple trees," says Molly. "They give privacy and I love the sheer beauty of them." The Drews' apples are sold to Knudsen, the Apple Farm, and Germain-Robin Alembic Brandy. As she talks about living and working on this beautiful spot on Greenwood Ridge, five Baby Doll sheep graze under the apple trees. "Lamb mowers," she said with a laugh. "They are descended from a heritage breed in the South Downs of Sussex."

She waves to her sons, Owen and Aidan, who run off to play with the neighbors. In the lower barn, Jason makes signature Pinot Noir and Syrah wines from California coastal grapes.

Both attended Los Altos High School on the Peninsula, south of San Francisco, but Molly and Jason didn't meet until after college. "I went to UC Santa Cruz and did a stint at St. Supery Winery in Napa Valley," he says. He got his degree in agro-ecology and then moved toward wine. "I became captivated," he remembers.

For the next eighteen years, Jason translated his captivation into "completing the circle of wine." In 1996, he and Molly married and moved to Anderson Valley where he was vineyard manager at Navarro Vineyards. Wanting to "get more serious in the wine arena," Jason decided to go to Australia where he earned a graduate degree in enology at the University of Adelaide. He and Molly lived in Australia for one and a half years and they had their first child, Owen, there.

They moved back to California where Jason went to work for several world-class wineries in Napa Valley. Next, they moved to Santa Barbara where Jason spent five years at Babcock Vineyards and got hooked on Syrah and Pinot Noir wines. He and Molly, who was a social worker, launched the Drew label in 2000.

"We wanted to buy land," says Jason, "and we felt our home is northern California and we had lived in Anderson Valley, which is prime agricultural land for Pinot Noir." They found this California Certified Organic property in 2004.

For most of 2005, the four Drews lived in a silver Bambi Airstream trailer while building the barn. They bathed the boys in grape bins. "Sometimes we would fill one of the giant galvanized bins with water and just soak in it after a hard day," Molly says, adding that the best moment of that year was when the washer and dryer were delivered.

Jason makes a Pinot Noir grown at Weir Vineyard in Yorkville Highlands. He adopted the Boontling word "Fog Eater" (which refers to those from the Coast) for Pinot Noir made from Anderson Valley vineyards including Monument Tree, which is about fourteen miles from the ocean. Drew's Syrah comes from Broken Leg Vineyard on the northwest side of Anderson Valley and the Ridgeline label comes from two vineyards from Mendocino Ridge appellation or AVA .

At the Drews' idyllic spot three miles from the Pacific, they are often above the fog that wraps around the base of the knoll. It's never too hot and doesn't experience the diurnal temperature swings you get in Anderson Valley. Its a perfect place for raising their children, apples, animals, and grapes.

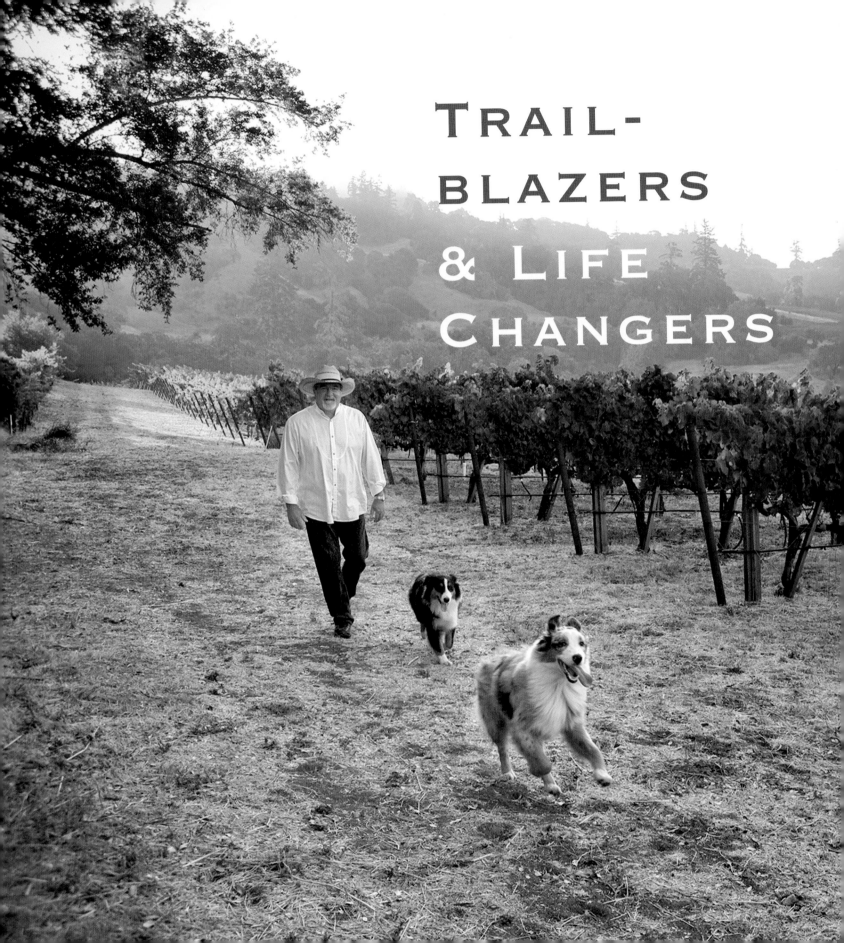

TRAIL-BLAZERS & LIFE CHANGERS

Mendocino's natural beauty, from roots to ridges, lures the intrepid looking for change and challenge. Newcomers to the wine business, such as those in this section, came from diverse careers including high-tech, social work, interior design and firefighting—rerooting themselves from urban lives to settle in rural Yorkville and Anderson Valley and become winemakers. Other people profiled in this book that have a trailblazing lifestyle are Guinness McFadden, a former navy officer who came to Potter Valley from Stanford Business School forty years ago, and Deborah Schatzlein, an environmental engineer from Colorado, now the winemaker at Bink. Stewart Bewley, creator of the wine cooler, is now growing Bordeaux varietals on his isolated mountaintop Alder Springs Vineyard, near Laytonville in northern Mendocino County.

CLAUDIA SPRINGS
HOME WINEMAKER TO PRO

PHILO RIDGE
OFF THE GRID AND LOVING IT

TOULOUSE VINEYARDS
PUNSTERS, WINE AND CUISINE

AT LEFT:

TOM RODRIGUES WITH BUSTER AND POSEY

CLAUDIA SPRINGS

HOME WINEMAKER TO PRO

A turkey runs along the fence as you make your way up the gravel road to Claudia Springs Winery in Anderson Valley. It's trying to get over to its flock, which is milling among the vines, nipping at the low-hanging grapes. Bob and Claudia Klindt are not turkey lovers. "They eat the grapes and are pesky intruders," they say.

In the twenty-plus years they have been grape growers and winemakers, the Klindts, who were career social workers, have learned to deal with turkeys and many other effects of their lifestyle change. Previously, Bob was an award-winning home winemaker in San Jose with aspirations to go professional.

One weekend in 1989, he cajoled Claudia and another couple, Claudia and Warren Hein, to enjoy a getaway to Mendocino County. They found this property for sale located about fifteen miles from the coast on the north side of Highway 128 in Anderson Valley.

"When Bob saw the one-thousand-gallon stainless-steel tank in the carport, he got excited," Claudia remembers, "and there was no turning back." The four friends purchased the twenty acres with a home on it from Milla Handley, who began Handley Cellars here in 1982. "We put up our house for sale in San Jose and sold it even before Milla accepted our offer," says Claudia.

With a startup kitty of $20,000, they wrote a business plan as they went along. Everyone sorted out his or her jobs to make their first release. "When we started," says Claudia, "we knew nothing about what it takes to produce commercial wine or even what a pallet jack was." In the beginning, they purchased six tons of Chardonnay grapes and Bob crushed them by himself. Shortly after they closed the deal, they produced 550 cases of Claudia Springs Chardonnay. The two Claudias inspired the winery's name and the foursome chose a fitting Maxfield Parrish scene of two ladies next to a gushing spring to put on the Claudia Springs label.

For the next five years, the Klindts commuted between their jobs in San Jose and their fledgling winery in Anderson Valley. When they found jobs with Mendocino County Social Services, they moved here full time. By 1998, eight acres of Pinot Noir and two acres of Pinot Gris grapes were planted. The Heins sold their share of the winery to the Klindts the same year.

In addition to their own grapes, the Klindts use grapes from many vineyards around Mendocino County. To show where the grapes are grown, a beautiful color-coded map hangs in their tasting room, which is located next to Floodgate Store on Highway 128. The zinc-topped tasting bar was originally in Bob's dad's soda fountain in Big Timber, Montana, where Bob was born and raised.

Retired from their county jobs, Bob and Claudia have more time to sit outside with friends under the shade of a forested slope next to their house. The cooling ocean air keeps the south-facing property from getting too hot and contributes to the slow ripening of their grapes. Claudia says, "This is a creative process for Bob." He responds, "I couldn't write or sing, but I found I was able to take some grapes and make something people enjoy."

PHILO RIDGE
OFF THE GRID AND LOVING IT

Since moving here full time in 2003, Heather McKelvey and Fred Buonanno jumped into a life off the grid to grow grapes and make wine. They have rehabilitated the old vines, barn and home, and put Philo Ridge Vineyards on the premium-wine map.

It hasn't been without challenges. During their transition from high-tech jobs in the Bay Area, they have been deluged by torrential rain, encircled by forest fires, and awakened by a mountain lion in their bedroom.

"When we moved to Anderson Valley, we knew nothing about farming or grapes," laughs Fred. "But we liked to drink wine," adds Heather. She has transformed her "dabbling in home winemaking" in their San Francisco garage to being Philo Ridge's award-winning winemaker.

Philo Ridge Vineyards, located five miles up a gravel road off Highway 128, is at 1,200 feet elevation. The energy to power their home and winery comes from the rays of the sun. The quiet is broken by Boo, a playful golden retriever rescue dog from Santa Rosa, who occasionally barks for someone to throw a stick.

The highest point on their beautiful, terraced property allows a 360-degree view. You can see from Low Gap Road winding to the north, to the Bald Hills of Navarro on the west, to Greenwood Ridge near the coast. In 2008, the couple watched as forest fires started by lightning strikes ignited around them. They saw five fires to the east grow together and three other fires blazing as they rushed to get their Gewurztraminer bottled. The Volunteer Fire Department advised Fred and Heather to evacuate; instead they helped as spotters and donated their pond water to fight the fires.

"We've learned a lot since we came here from the corporate world," laughs Fred, who gave up his old life traveling 200,000 miles a year setting up global distribution channels for a high-tech company. Heather still works as an engineer at a software company in Petaluma. Fred had to learn to drive a tractor. "We both learned how to repair pipes," says Heather.

"Our first year, we lost half the crop to the turkeys and occasional bears," says Fred. They planted manzanita and huckleberry borders to keep the turkeys distracted, and net the rows once the fruit begins to ripen. High posts made from logs culled on the sixty-six-acre property are placed along the rows to anchor the netting. For fire protection, they created a defensible space that is meticulously cared for around the vineyard and buildings.

They re-contoured the vineyard terraces to make wider row spacing and added natural plant borders between them. Heather and Fred added a deck wide enough to accommodate a vegetable garden and refurbished their solar-powered home.

Fred has remodeled the old barn for their winery, keeping the original tree poles and redwood beams. The focus of the winery is their acclaimed Pinot Noir. Heather and Fred are drawn to a fruit-forward and light-oak-on-the-finish style of winemaking. Their Vino di Mendocino, which includes Zinfandel, Syrah, Petite Sirah and Carignane, is an example. They have also joined Coro Mendocino. In the spring of 2011, Fred and Heather opened a lively and beautifully decorated tasting room in downtown Boonville.

Their rural living adventures continue. One night they awoke to the sounds of trouble downstairs. When Fred got up to investigate, he discovered fresh blood on the dining room floor. At the same time, Heather watched a baby mountain lion chase her injured cat through the bedroom and out the window. "The mountain lion got Gabby in the paw and had her head in its mouth, but, miraculously, it dropped her." In addition to taking Gabby to the vet, they headed to the animal shelter and came home with Boo.

"These are not the kinds of experiences we had in our former lives," says Heather.

> HAVING A MOUNTAIN LION COME THROUGH YOUR BEDROOM WINDOW AND RUN OUT WITH YOUR CAT IS NOT AN EXPERIENCE WE HAD IN OUR URBAN LIVES.
>
> —HEATHER MCKELVEY, PHILO RIDGE VINEYARDS

TOULOUSE VINEYARDS
PUNSTERS, WINE AND CUISINE

The sign with a punster's slogan and stately goose illustration marks the entrance to Toulouse Vineyards off Highway 128, just north of Philo in Anderson Valley. A meandering driveway leads to the crush-pad parking area where an olive orchard borders the two-story barn, which doubles as the winery and residence of the owners, Vern and Maxine Boltz.

The goose on the sign and Toulouse's wine labels is a conversation starter at the handcrafted bar in the tasting room next to the barn. "Too tense?" reads the sign (and the T-shirt). "Toulouse" (pronounced "too loose") is the answer.

In 1997, when Vern retired from the Oakland Fire Department, he bought the 160-acre ranch just around the bend from downtown Philo and has since added another 160 acres. "I planted twenty acres in Pinot Noir and one in Riesling," he says

"Vern is the dreamer," says Maxine, who was a flight attendant for twenty-five years and then in real estate in the Bay Area. "I never know what to expect when he says, 'You know what I want to do next?'" For now, Vern is the winemaker and bottling line boss. A part-time contractor during his years as a firefighter, Vern remodeled the upstairs of the barn into living quarters. He is also responsible for fence mending and winery alterations. "Vern does it all," says Maxine.

"In 2002, when our first crop was ready to harvest commercially," says Vern, "the grape market was down, so we decided to make wine." He and Maxine wanted to put an animal on the label. "We liked the names Duckhorn and Frog's Leap," Vern explains. Then they learned about the classic big gray breed known as the Toulouse goose.

Vern and Maxine have fun with name Toulouse depending upon how you pronounce it, as in, "What have we got Toulouse (to lose)? Or, "You drink too much and you get Toulouse." It didn't take long to adopt "Too tense? Toulouse" as a motto. In the tasting room, they keep a copy of renowned journalist and essayist Mort Rosenblum's book, *A Goose in Toulouse and Other Culinary Adventures in France*.

At the tasting bar made from a redwood plank set on wine barrels, it doesn't take long to understand why the wines are such winners. The first vintage, a 2002 Toulouse Pinot Noir, made the *San Francisco Chronicle*'s list of the top one hundred wines for 2005. Toulouse Pinot Noir has also been named among the "world's thirty best Pinot Noirs" by *Food & Wine* magazine.

The Boltzes have added a Rosé of Pinot Noir, Riesling from their estate grown grapes, Gewurztraminer from Valley Foothills Vineyard and Pinot Gris from Corby Vineyard, all in Anderson Valley. Occasionally they also make Cabernet Sauvignon.

"These wines are great with all kinds of food flavors," says Maxine. "With our Pinot Gris, have something that is seasoned with a little lemon or lime. You want the food to be slightly less sweet and acidic than the wine," she explains. Maxine partnered with Chef Dory Kwan to help create culinary and wine education events. Dory also develops recipes to go with Toulouse wines.

Anytime the goose sign is at the open gate on Highway 128, the tasting room is open. "We're a little winery but we have a great time," say Maxine and Vern. What have you got Tou-louse?

VALUE ADDED

The vineyards and wineries profiled here have taken winemaking to another level. Diversifying their crops, keeping an ear on the market and developing new ways to continue to live off the land and support Mendocino viticulture are the motives of these especially enterprising people. They bring added value to the Mendocino wine industry and are leaders in sustainability as well as marketing.

McFADDEN FARM
GRAPES, HERBS, GARLIC, ENERGY

DNA VINEYARDS
WHEN DENNIS MET ANDREA

TERRA SÁVIA
SYMBIOSIS OF WINE AND OLIVES

RACK & RIDDLE
FIRST AND SECONDARY FERMENTATION

MCFADDEN FARM

GRAPES, HERBS, GARLIC, ENERGY

Forty years ago, Guinness McFadden combined his business sense with a penchant for anticipating trends in the California food, wine and energy scene. As the proprietor of McFadden Farm in Potter Valley he splits his time among farming, winemaking, marketing and running a small power plant.

A grape grower since the early 1970s, Guinness started producing wine under his own label in 2003. For decades, he has grown and bottled his line of McFadden Farm dried herbs and herb blends with the distinctive California quail on the label. In addition, he packages wild rice and raises organic beef.

"Farming this place gives me a thrill," says Guinness. "I know it's not really 'mine.' My role is to take care of the beautiful property while I'm here." Guinness didn't want to raise his kids where a lot of chemicals were used, so MacFadden Farm became California Certified Organic in 1990.

Guinness, a native New Yorker, Notre Dame graduate and ex-naval officer with a stint at Stanford's business school, came to Mendocino as a "back-to-the-lander." A photo in McFadden Farm's tasting room in Hopland shows a young man with longish dark hair sitting on the dilapidated steps to the old farmhouse that is his home.

His since remodeled farmhouse sits atop a knoll. It has a full-length south-facing sun porch and country kitchen with a restaurant-sized Wolf range. A New England-style covered bridge crosses the

Russian River next to the powerhouse Guinness built twenty-five years ago, generating power for about half of the west side of Potter Valley. Three hundred solar panels line the top of a giant shed roof, next to the herb dryers, creating thirty-seven kilowatts of electricity.

Today, McFadden Farm encompasses 500 acres. There are 160 acres of vineyards planted with Riesling, Sauvignon Blanc, Pinot Gris, Gewurztraminer, Pinot Noir and Zinfandel grapes. Ten acres of herbs include oregano, rosemary, basil, marjoram, lemon thyme and thyme.

There is always something to do at the farm. In the fall, the herb-drying equipment is put to use. "We come into the warehouse on rainy days and pack and label the herbs, one jar at a time," says Guinness. The herb business helps keep everyone employed year round. In addition to processing and packing the herb blends, he and his crew also braid 50,000 pounds of garlic and make bay wreaths for the holidays and Williams-Sonoma catalogs.

Guinness, now in his seventies, admits he is not living the life of retirement, but says he takes time to walk around the farm remembering all the steps he had to take to get here. "You plant, watch it grow, harvest, and make wine. This is the best job a guy can have."

DNA VINEYARDS
WHEN DENNIS MET ANDREA

DNA Vineyards, their company, is named for Dennis Patton and Andrea Silverstein. Dennis sources bulk wine made in Mendocino County to blend and create new labels for customers. At times their living room is lined with up to 200 bottles of sample wines, which Dennis tastes and blends to each of their clients' specifications. Andrea works with designers to put together the packaging and she tracks shipments and invoices, case lots and inventory. They work with small wine orders, and for large ones such as for Trader Joe's.

The two have known each other since the 1980s and married in 2004. They work from home five miles southwest of Ukiah while raising their daughter Samantha.

He was a back-to-the-land hippie. She was destined for a life in medicine like her father, uncles and brothers. He has a passion for growing things and a talented sense of taste. She has curiosity and an aptitude for business. His ingenuity and labors over the last forty years destined him to become one of Mendocino County's most renowned and quotable winemakers. Her creativity and energy blazed a path into the world of wine entrepreneurship.

Dennis has made wine in Mendocino County since the late 1970s. He knows the growers and what their fruit is like. He also has the palate and intuition to know when to buy wine or juice. "I know where the good grapes are in the county and I want to see them get used," he says.

A winemaker who has always used grapes grown by others, Dennis has his own vineyard for the first time. He and Andrea planted four acres in 2006. Their certified organic Grenache Noir, Syrah, Petite Sirah and Zinfandel vines slope down the northeast facing bowl in a semicircle with a pond at the base. For someone who has worked with every varietal grown in the region, Dennis chose these grapes because "they ripen easily even at our 1,400 to 1,550 foot elevation because of the amount of time the sun shines on them."

Dennis, who grew up in suburban San Jose, relocated to Mendocino County in 1975 when his younger brother, David, mentioned he had friends with an option on a ranch near Ukiah. "We all piled into a hippie VW van and drove up Highway 101 to find this beautiful property on Greenfield Ranch," say Dennis, who with his brother bought into a fifty-acre parcel.

"I had my feet in the land and came up here to grow stuff," he says. He was soon meeting grape growers and people in the wine business and taking classes in winemaking at UC Davis. He networked with John Scharffenberger who was starting his sparkling wine business in Ukiah at the time.

"I was one of the first certified organic farmers in Mendocino County," says Dennis. He began winemaking with eighty gallons of Carignane, Zinfandel and Cabernet Sauvignon. By 1981, Dennis and a group of friends became partners and bonded Hidden Cellars Winery, which was located on Mill Creek Road. After the winery sold twenty years later, Dennis began a consulting business and had no shortage of clients.

In the meantime, in the mid-1980s, Dennis met Andrea at a wine event in Los Angeles. "I looked at this guy dressed in a silk paisley shirt with this big curly head of hair and I thought what a freak, but he sure makes great wine," she laughs. Andrea, who was exporting wine to Japan at the time, became intrigued with the Mendocino wine story.

Now this couple combines Dennis's renowned winemaking skills with Andrea's administrative, marketing and sales abilities. Their reputation has helped them land contracts with big natural grocery outlets. "We are truly in a niche," says Silverstein. DNA Vineyards produces high quality wine of great value and their customers know what they will get as Patton showcases his old friends' Mendocino vineyards.

"We could do our business more economically somewhere else, but we love it here," says Silverstein, who plays the cello in the Ukiah Symphony and takes ballet classes. Quoting Mark Twain who said, "Youth is wasted on the young," Patton isn't slowing down. He laughed and said, "I'm about as smart as a teenager now." Some of DNA's labels include Rootstock, TBD and Captain's Catch for such retailers as Trader Joe's.

TERRA SÁVIA

SYMBIOSIS OF WINE AND OLIVES

"I'm the wine guy, she is the olive gal," begins Jim Milone. He and Yvonne Hall are sitting at the handmade redwood-slab picnic table inside the vast wine tasting/olive oil-pressing warehouse on the south end of Hopland. This is home to Terra Sávia Winery and Olivino Olive Press

Jim has been making wine in Mendocino County for nearly three decades. He and his wife Vicki live in the family home, adjacent to the vineyard that surrounds the warehouse/tasting room/olive press. Tall with a shock of graying wavy hair, Jim has deep roots in Mendocino County. His Italian great-grandfather, Achille Rosetti, had a winery across the Sanel Valley before it was shut down during Prohibition.

Jim grew up working in the vineyards alongside his father and grandfather. "I heard about grapes and wine from my family every day," he remembers. "We raised our food and made our own wine in this same vicinity for generations."

"The way I and many of us who live around here grew up is not so common these days," says Jim "I was brought up like families have been forever in Italy and other parts of the world."

In 1975, he and Greg Graziano started the Milano Winery. "It was the first winery in Hopland after Prohibition," he says. At the time, there were only eight wineries in Mendocino County. He sold Milano Winery in 2001 to Ted and Deanna Starr.

Both Terra Sávia's vineyards and nearby olive orchard with 2,500 Tuscan varietal trees subscribe to Fish Friendly Farming practices and are California Certified Organic Farms. Even the name of the wine, Terra Sávia, was carefully chosen. It means "wise earth." One percent of the sales of Terra Sávia wine supports Wildlife Rescue.

"We are not making trophy wines," says Milone, whose goal is to make good wine affordable. His Terra Sávia Meritage includes Bordeaux varietals and is a smooth mouthful with layers of flavors. He also makes Petite Verdot as a stand-alone wine. Other Terra Sávia wines include a refreshing non-oaked Chardonnay, purple and vibrant Petite Verdot, luscious Cabernet Sauvignon, a small amount of a single block vineyard Pinot Noir, and a Rosé sparkling wine.

Terra Sávia and Olivino wine and olive oil are produced on site in a naturally timed symbiosis. After the grapes are harvested and crushed, the focus turns to olive oil. While the wine is settling

and relatively dormant in the winter months, the olive oil takes center stage. Two stainless steel olive presses are put to use in November and December. Olives from Olivino and other local olive growers are gently crushed and squeezed into the prized oil.

In the cavernous tasting room, sitting areas with handcrafted chairs, benches and picnic tables, some by local craftsman Ben Frey, and a Persian rug and Victorian couches, create cozy salon-like areas. The slab tables gracefully incorporate black walnut, redwood and other woods. Terra Sávia wines and olive oil, including Classic Tuscan, Pure Moraiolo and Pure Leccino are on the tasting menu. Museum quality art work graces the wide high walls.

Outside, there's a greenhouse and olive trees in pots everywhere. Olive trees are for sale. They take between three and five years to make enough of a crop for the olives to be pressed into oil.

Summing up their business philosophy, Jim says, "Our parallel philosophy is that we are thoughtful, organic by default, and we gauge every decision by how it will affect others—a precautionary principle in practice."

RACK & RIDDLE

FIRST AND SECONDARY FERMENTATION

Rack & Riddle fills a niche in the wine world. Opened in Hopland in 2007 by two entrepreneurs who began their careers in champagne-style sparkling wine production, Rack & Riddle is set up to handle a million gallons of custom-made sparkling and still wine.

"Because you don't have to buy your own equipment, hire winemakers and store the wine, you can save tens of thousands of dollars at a custom crush facility like ours," says Bruce Lundquist who, with Rebecca Faust, are partners in Rack & Riddle.

Custom crush services in the certified organic facility include crushing the grapes, fermentation, barrel aging, and bottling. They also offer case storage. In other words, they take care of everything from press to bottle, and from racking the still wines to riddling the sparklers.

Rebecca dreamed of being her own boss while working at other wineries. Bruce, who grew up in the Tillamook region of Oregon, always wanted to be a farmer. As professional colleagues, they shared their aspirations and began looking around at a possible site. When they found the former Duncan Peak storage facility for sale in Hopland they wondered what they could do with the 120,000 square feet of buildings.

"What we saw here was wine storage," says Bruce, the gregarious accountant and former partner of Longboard Vineyards, whose wines are now made at Rack & Riddle.

Bruce and Rebecca started working on a business plan incorporating their respective sparkling wine experiences and filling a need they observed in the wine industry. Synchronistically, an opportunity arose that spurred them on.

They made a winning bid on the contract to make Bearboat Wine, which was being sold by Remy Martin Company. "Things fell into place like dominoes," recalls Rebecca, adding, "It was a wild ride that first year."

"We were thinking small scale," says Rebecca. Before they knew it, they were committed to 100,000 cases of wine. "We were out on a limb and wondering, is there a trunk?"

There was no time to ponder. They jumped into financing, equipment purchases, real estate closure, other client contracts and all the usual pieces it takes to start a business from utilities to employees. Over the spring and summer of 2007, they renovated the facility, purchased winemaking equipment and applied for organic certification of the entire place.

Located at the south end of Hopland off Mountain House Road, Rack & Riddle sits back from the road under the towering Duncan Peak to the west. The 17,000-square-foot crush pad can accommodate anything from one-ton trucks to twenty-ton semis.

When their neighbor drives his tractor pulling small bins on a trailer, he gets in line for his weigh tag sandwiched between eighteen-wheelers. "We are as welcoming to small growers as we are to the driver with 40,000 pounds in one load," says Rebecca.

Temperature-controlled stainless tanks, barrel storage, lab facilities and advanced technology are among their services. They employ winemakers with a range of experience. "We cover the spectrum—sparkling, still, boutique and large lots—with our good mix of industry vets who are excellent winemakers," says Rebecca. They make sparkling wine for McFadden, Paul Dolan and other Mendocino growers.

Rack & Riddle's location off Highway 101 makes it ideal for custom crushing grapes from all over the North Coast. Their tasting room features Rack & Riddle's own sparkling and other wines.

"We are on track to be of service to the surrounding wine vicinity," say Bruce and Rebecca, "and we appreciate being part of the green footprint that defines Mendocino County."

PURELY PINOT

Anderson Valley's reputation for excellent Pinot Noir helped put Mendocino County on California's wine map three decades ago. Now Anderson Valley hosts a three-day Pinot Noir Festival every May, attracting hundreds of Pinot lovers. Warm days and cool nights make for ideal growing conditions for this finicky grape, which was planted in the early 1970s by luminaries such as Navarro, Lazy Creek, Husch, and Edmeades. In the 1980s, the French Champagne house Louis Roederer chose Anderson Valley to expand its holdings to the United States, finding the climate and terroir perfect for méthode champenoise sparkling wine grapes such as Pinot. Pinot Noir is found in nearly every winery along Highway 128 in Anderson Valley. While the three featured wineries specialize in Pinot Noir, more Pinot Noir wineries in other sections include Shandel's Oppenlander, Baxter, Handley, Navarro, Lula, Barra, Masut, Graziano, and Naughty Boy.

Even more are listed on www.mendowine.com. In addition, noteworthy out-of-county wineries such as Littorai, La Crema, Copain, Cakebread, Saintsbury, Woodenhead, and Black Kite use Pinot Noir grown around Anderson Valley. You'll also find excellent Pinot produced by Mendocino's Hopland, Redwood Valley and Potter Valley wineries.

GOLDENEYE
REACHING PINOT PERFECTION

ELKE
WINE OF A PLACE

PHILLIPS HILL
ART AND PINOT

PINOT GRAPES - REDWOOD VALLEY

GOLDENEYE

REACHING PINOT PERFECTION

Goldeneye is the study of a varietal in an appellation. Focusing on Pinot Noir provides Goldeneye the ability to make wine that is an expression of its place. Most of Goldeneye's five vineyards in Anderson Valley are on hillsides. Goldeneye has been producing Pinot Noir in Anderson Valley since 1996 when the Duckhorns from Napa Valley purchased the former Obester Vineyard and Winery.

While appreciative of France's Burgundy, the winemakers of Goldeneye describe their Pinot Noir as having characteristics that can only be achieved by the land and climate here. "We are engaged with what we have," says former winemaker Zach Rasmussen. Each vintage Goldeneye Pinot Noir is "the most perfect blend from Anderson Valley we can make."

The winemakers work with nearly a hundred individual lots sorted by vineyard block, Choosing lots of wine from the top down. When a wine from a particular vineyard stands out, it receives a designated label.

Duckhorn's other Pinot Noir label is Migration, with an emphasis on wines with vibrancy and finesse. Migration showcases the red fruit elements of Pinot Noir that mean a lighter range with bright raspberry, strawberry or cherry flavors.

Goldeneye's tasting room is in a craftsman-style house that is as inviting outside as it is comfortable inside. Mission furniture, stained-glass light fixtures and a scattering of duck decoys set a warm, welcoming atmosphere where there is no traditional tasting bar. Instead, happy tasters often occupy an oak dining table inside or a picnic table on the patio. Picture windows on east and west walls zoom in on surrounding vineyards.

Goldeneye Anderson Valley Pinot Noir and Migration Anderson Valley Pinot Noir are available for tasting for a nominal fee. With each wine, the taster receives an oversized coaster-like label with the wine's growing, harvesting and technical information on the back, along with comments from the winemakers. Tasters also receive a food sampling, which may include such tidbits as roasted almonds, slivers of Fiscalini San Joaquin Gold cheese and dried sour cherries.

Up the road from the tasting room is Goldeneye's LEED (Leadership in Energy and Environmental Design) certified winery. It was designed for the kind of small-lot winemaking and blending they do at Goldeneye. Accolades for Goldeneye appear regularly in the wine press and the wines are found at the best restaurants and dining tables. When Goldeneye Pinot Noir was poured at the United States Senate's luncheon for President Obama's 2009 inauguration, it reached a pinnacle.

ELKE VINEYARDS
WINE OF A PLACE

"Growing grapes and making wine are tangible, heartfelt ways to spend time," says Mary Elke. "Plus I meet the most interesting people."

Mary Elke is a grape and apple grower with acreage in two Anderson Valley locations and another in Napa Valley. Known for years for her Mary Elke Apple Juice, she also makes Pinot Noir and Chardonnay.

She and her husband purchased the Napa Valley parcel and planted grapes, including Pinot Noir, in the 1970s "long before it was the chichi place it is today," she says. The vineyard was supposed to pay off by the time their two boys went to college and be the source of college tuition. "Instead," she says, "phylloxera hit the Napa vineyards and we ended up taking out loans to replant the vineyard and pay for college."

From years of experience, Elke has developed a distinct philosophy about growing grapes. "If you orient the vines the right way, practice good viticulture and have appropriate trellising, you will produce 'wine of a place,'" she explains. Her goal is to produce more tons per acre than is customary for Pinot Noir. She developed a pruning system that allows the fruit to grow across the canopy in a way that equally ripens most clusters. "I'm bucking the common learning," she says, noting that the smaller yield philosophy "is not yet scientifically proven."

Anyone can make good wine out of lower yields, says Mary. She wants to show you can make good wine from higher yields. "The grapevine wants to grow and produce as much fruit as it can ripen," she says. "It wants to make more grapes than two tons per acre, and if the conditions are right and the vine is in balance it easily can."

In 1997, Mary made her first commercial production of Elke Pinot Noir. Now the winery produces up to 1,800 cases and includes some production of Chardonnay and a limited quantity of Pinot Noir Rosé.

She describes her Pinot Noir as "more feminine, layered and nuanced" compared with Pinots from the Russian River or the Central Coast. "It is less fruit driven with better acidity. I think it's what Pinot Noir should taste like," she says. She places a sign in front of the vineyard on Highway 128 in Anderson Valley just north of Boonville to let you know Elke is open for tasting.

PHILLIPS HILL ESTATES
ART AND PINOT

"People say 'Wow' when they come in and find I only have Pinot Noir," says Toby Hill, winemaker and proprietor of Phillips Hill Estates.

The former real estate office with the blooming clematis-covered porch has been transformed by winemaker-proprietor Toby Hill into an artisan's den that is perfect for tasting his vineyard designated Pinot Noir wines.

Toby, with boyish good looks and a genial manner, mans the tasting bar. Framed prints of Phillips Hill wine labels created from Toby's abstract lithographs and drawings adorn the walls. Wine-barrel end tables, a row of connected wooden church hall chairs, and comfy rattan stools are the only furniture in the muted yellow room with its painted wainscot ceiling.

Actually Toby also makes a little rosé from Pinot Noir as well as Gewurztraminer to whet your palate, but the main focus is Pinot Noir. Each Phillips

Hill Pinot Noir is made from a specific vineyard in Anderson Valley or nearby Comptche. "The Shandel's Oppenlander vineyard a few miles west of Comptche is a secret little find," says Toby.

Toby's journey to winemaker involved an innate sense of taste, serendipity and being open to what was dealt his way. Born in San Francisco, Toby was raised in Manhattan, returned to the Bay Area to go to California College of Arts and Crafts, and returned to New York where he lived the life of a successful artist.

Relocating to San Francisco in 1989, he had a studio in the emerging Hunters Point artist's enclave. One weekend he came to Mendocino County to visit his best friend from high school at his family's place in Comptche.

"I immediately thought it would be nice to have a place up here in the country," he says. It wasn't long before he found thirty acres on Greenwood Ridge. He built a barn with an artist's studio, and he packed up and moved to Mendocino County.

When he was offered four barrels of unfinished Pinot Noir wine in 2001, he changed direction. "If anyone had asked if I would become a winemaker ten years ago, I would have said they were crazy," he remembers. Here was someone born in San Francisco and raised in Manhattan, an urban artist with a successful import business. "It's great how life just evolves its own way," he says.

Toby made one hundred cases from those first four barrels, which he released in 2002. He renovated his art studio into a winery and now his art is focused on Pinot Noir wine labels. In addition to a couple of vintages from Oppenlander Vineyard, Toby makes Phillips Hill Pinot Noir from Toulouse Vineyard up the road in Anderson Valley, Corby Vineyard on the east side of the Navarro River and Marguerite Vineyard on Holmes Ranch, also in Anderson Valley.

Toby named his winery for his grandmother, whose maiden name was Phillips. "Wine is an art form," says Toby. The character of each wine inspires the Phillips Hill labels. At ease sharing his art with the people who walk in, he describes running the tasting room as like having an open studio every day.

"It's great to showcase these vineyards and be part of a region growing amazing full-bodied grapes," says Toby.

FRENCH CONNECTIONS

Early in the 1970s, winemakers discovered that grapes from the Rhône, Champagne and Alsace wine regions in France have an affinity with Mendocino County's soil and climate. Varietals such as Pinot Noir and Chardonnay from Burgundy and Champagne, and Gewurztraminer and Riesling from Alsace, grow well in Anderson Valley's cool nights and warm days. Syrah and Grenache reach their lively fruit-forward potential in warmer inland areas such as McDowell Valley near Hopland where one-hundred-year-old vines still produce. They also do well on hilltop vineyards such as Eaglepoint Ranch and in blocks in Ukiah, Redwood and Potter Valleys. The following examples of Mendocino's French connections feature a French champagne company that found a place to grow grapes to the standards of their native Champagne; a Francophile who loves the grapes of the Rhône; and the French hitchhiker from a 300-year-old cognac-distilling family.

Another section titled *Bordeaux in Mendo* profiles three wineries that focus on the wines of another of France's famed wine regions. For more information on Alsatian varietals, see Navarro from Anderson Valley, where the winegrowers host an International Alsace Varietals Festival each February.

ROEDERER ESTATE
MÉTHODE CHAMPENOISE

BAXTER
FRENCH FLAVOR FROM MENDO GRAPES

GERMAIN-ROBIN
WORLD CLASS BRANDY

BRANDY BARRELS, GERMAIN-ROBIN

MÉTHODE CHAMPENOISE

From the distinctive stone gate to the tasting room with its high ceilings, French fabrics, 250-year-old Bordeaux floor tiles and the French glass champagne flutes, the décor is unmistakably French at Roederer Estate in Anderson Valley.

The story begins in 1776, when the family-owned House of Champagne Louis Roederer was founded and began producing world-class champagne including the world's most expensive Cristal. Fast-forward to 1981, and the Louis Roederer history moves in a new direction when

across two continents and the Atlantic Ocean, Roederer Estate was established in Anderson Valley in Mendocino County.

"I feel a part of the family legacy," says Arnaud Weyrich, winemaker and vice president at Roederer Estate. Weyrich, a native of Alsace, is Roederer Estate's second winemaker. He moved to Anderson Valley with his family in 2000.

When the Louis Roederer company, which is still family-owned, sought a place to expand its holdings, it settled on this site less than twenty miles from the coast on Highway 128 in Anderson Valley. The site was found perfectly suited for Pinot Noir and Chardonnay, the classic Champagne grapes.

Weyrich oversees winemaking at Roederer Estate, which produces méthode champenoise sparkling wine just as its parent company has for more than 200 years. In the United States, champagne is known as "sparkling wine" out of respect to the French province of Champagne, where champagne originated and is the only place it is called champagne (save a few grandfathered exceptions).

"Sparkling wine is complicated. It needs direction and guidance," says Weyrich. There are a lot of operations. "Still wine is fermented one time. It is aged, bottled and shipped to the market," explains Weyrich. "I do two fermentations, one in the tank and one in the bottle."

In order to produce bubbles, which happens in the bottle, the wine destined to be a sparkler gets what is known as a "dosage," a slightly sweet addition, to help start a second fermentation in the bottle. For two and a half years the bottle is "riddled" or turned slowly on giant riddling racks to keep the yeast from sticking in one place. In the old days it was riddled by hand, and someone turned each bottle an eighth of a turn over and over. Today sophisticated machines turn the wine. Grapes picked for sparkling wine take at least three years before the finished wine is released.

Roederer makes a non-vintage Brut and a Brut Rosé, which has the palest salmon-colored blush. In addition, Weyrich oversees the production of the higher end L'Ermitage Brut and L'Ermitage Brut Rosé, made from the best wine or cuvée, which is what wine destined to become champagne is called. L'Ermitage is aged in the bottle for five years.

While Arnaud and his family are settled into the American way of life in Anderson Valley, Weyrich adds authenticity to the French feeling that comes with a visit to Roederer Estate. "We are keeping the traditions," he says. Most of the same crew has been at Roederer for years. In addition to the continuity of staff, Weyrich brings in interns from the French university he attended in Montpelier.

Roederer Estate is a pleasant interlude with a touch of France that integrates naturally with surrounding vineyards and Mendocino's coastal forests and oak-studded hillsides.

BAXTER WINERY

FRENCH FLAVOR FROM MENDO GRAPES

"I make wine the way I learned in Burgundy," says Phillip Baxter, Jr., winemaker at Baxter Winery, which straddles a knoll on Greenwood Ridge.

The setting encompasses a stunning view of Signal Ridge, where wisps of lightning fires smoked the horizon for more than a month in June 2008.

Phil, Jr., fit and boyishly handsome, was impressed with their good luck when he counted 200 lightning strikes the night of the storm. He did have to put off bottling when the smoke was at its thickest. "We lost two to three weeks of work," he says, "but our entire ridge was spared."

When the Baxter family purchased twenty-four acres on Greenwood Ridge in 2000, they put in a winery. Phil's father, Phil Sr., has been in the wine business in Napa Valley for more than forty years. In addition to working for other wineries Phillip Sr. helped start Rutherford Hill Winery, where he was chief winemaker for ten years.

Phil Jr. studied winemaking at the University of California at Davis. He spent a year in Burgundy in southeastern France and then went back to France after college to work the harvest in Pommard, famous for Côte de Beaune, in France's Burgundy wine region.

Baxter's tasting bar in the remodeled barn is an upended wine barrel. The "cellar" is stacked floor to ceiling with wine barrels "all purchased used," says Phil who likes to age his wines a year and a half in neutral French barrels so as not to pick up overpowering oak flavors. Cases of wine are stacked between the barrels.

Influenced by the flavors of Burgundy, especially the Northern Rhône and Côte Roti, Phil says, "I let my wines make themselves as much as possible." He ferments the grapes on their natural yeasts and leaves the wines unfined and unfiltered. His goal is to take advantage of the grapes from each vineyard he works with and "let nature do its thing, allowing the individual fruit characteristics to shine."

Phil makes about 2,500 cases of handcrafted Baxter wines and 200 cases under the Pipo label, a less expensive bistro wine. While the Baxter label is straightforward and classic, the Pipo labels feature charming sketches of French scenes. The Pipo Red label pictures a game of boules (French bocce) and is a blend of Carignane, Grenache, Zinfandel and Petite Sirah. The dry fruit-rich Pipo Rosé has a jeune fille on a scooter heading uphill to a Provençal village, "probably to a party," he says.

Phil Jr. also continues his family's Philippe-Lorraine, a 500-case brand started by his father Phil Sr., which is named after his French great-grandparents, Philippe and Lorraine Segrais.

In the laissez faire ambience of Baxter Winery life is about as good as it gets. "Work is fun and we eat and drink well," Phil says, tasting Baxter's 2006 Oppenlander Vineyards Pinot Noir. "Every time I taste this wine, I am back in Burgundy—probably because it captures the flavor that harkens to the vineyard. It's neither intense nor something that needs correcting, it is the flavor profile I am shooting for."

GERMAIN-ROBIN
WORLD-CLASS BRANDY

Germain-Robin brandy is produced by the same method as French cognac. Wine critics such as Dan Berger have considered it as possibly the world's finest cognac. The Redwood Valley distillery, founded in 1981, is discreetly located in a vineyard. The cognac-style brandy is meticulously handcrafted in a 650-gallon French copper still.

While the hands-on distillation procedures are the same here as they are in France, differences at Germain-Robin begin with the grapes and the wine being used. In Cognac, Ugni Blanc is the typical grape for the base wine. When Hubert Germain-Robin and Ansley Coale founded Germain-Robin at an old sheep ranch on Low Gap Road near Ukiah, the palate of possibilities with so many locally available grape varieties inspired Hubert.

Hubert is descended from a family that has produced cognac since 1782. He and his wife Carole came to California in the 1970s to find a place to continue the craft. When they first met Ansley, he was commuting between Berkeley, where he was a history professor, and his 2,000-acre ranch in Mendocino. Hubert went back to France and located a beautiful copper still and had it shipped to the ranch.

It would be four years before the first Germain-Robin brandy would be bottled and released. With no Ugni Blanc (also known at Trebbiano) around, they tapped another Cognac classic, French Colombard. Over the years, Hubert selected vineyards and directed the winemaking from Semillon, Sauvignon Blanc, Pinot Noir, Riesling, Viognier, Petite Sirah and Zinfandel grapes. Hubert, a master distiller, handcrafted the distilling and blending of the cognac-style brandy until 2009, when he handed on the duties to Joe Corley.

"In the beginning, my olfactory capabilities were honed to wine," says Joe, who now runs the distillery. "This was a whole new game," he shares. "I had a nose for the new challenge and was really excited about my work. I think Hubert saw that in me." He spends long hours working alone, tending the primary ten-hour and second twelve-hour distilling processes which take place during the winter months. "We get one gallon of brandy for every nine gallons of wine that is distilled," says Joe. The

rest of the year he shepherds the brandies from new oak barrels—all French-made from Limousin—to older barrels, keeping each wine lot separate until the time for blending.

"There is an incredible amount of detail work," Joe says. Germain-Robin produces about 3,000 cases at the distillery, which moved to Redwood Valley in 1999. In a cool storage room next to the still, 1,200 oak barrels are stored, each with its contents noted in chalk on the barrel end.

Among the brandies made at Germain-Robin, the youngest and most economical is the six- to seven-year-old Craft Method Brandy, also known as Fine Alambic Brandy. From there Germain-Robin brandies move up in price per bottle with aging and other special care and blending. They include in order of aging: XO, Coast Road Reserve, Single Barrel and Anno Domini (which sells for upward of $300).

Germain-Robin also makes single varietal grappa, a clear brandy made from such wines as Pinot Noir, Viognier, Muscat or Zinfandel. This grappa has round smooth flavors and not the harsh bite some grappas are known for. Germain-Robin Apple Brandy is sourced from Mendocino orchards such as Drew. A local favorite after-dinner liqueur is

Crème de Poete, based on Petite Sirah wine infused with nuts and dried fruits. Each bottling is slightly different and each has a poem on the label.

Inhaling the aromas of fine cognac-style brandy is like taking a fermentation tour of the last two or three decades of Mendocino winemaking. Learning to appreciate fine brandy is a practiced art and corroborates Germain-Robin's mission, which, says Joe Corley, "is to take wine to its higher purpose."

CULTURE SHIFT

Throughout history, nearly every culture on the planet fermented something to drink. While evidence exists showing wine was made as early as 6,000 years ago in the Middle East, grape wine has been the domain of Mediterranean Europeans for 2,000 years. Today, wine is produced in more than seventy countries from South Africa to New Zealand, Canada to Argentina, Great Britain to Kyrgyzstan. In the twentieth century, we began to see wine paired with every type of cuisine whether it comes from Asia, Africa, northern Europe or Latin America and whether or not the culture has a prior wine tradition. In Mendocino County, three vintners stand out for changing stereotypes and blending their Mexican/Hispanic, Filipina, and African American heritages into their winemaking.

SIMAINE CELLARS
ORGANIC SINGLE
VINEYARD VARIETALS

CESAR TOXQUI
MULTI-HERITAGE HEIRLOOMS

ESTERLINA
DREAMS OF A FATHER

SIMAINE CELLARS

ORGANIC SINGLE-VINEYARD VARIETALS

In 2005, culling from the fruits of his many years in the wine business, Victor Simon, native of Mexico, started a winery with his wife Brenda.

"Victor and I became friends working together at the former Fife Winery above Lake Mendocino. Our relationship developed and he became part of my family," says Brenda, a Ukiah native whose maiden name is Maine. The winery is named Simaine to combine both of their family names. It is pronounced "Sy' mane."

Victor credits his upbringing and his grandparents for introducing him to wine. Born in Mexico City, Victor went to live at a young age with his grandparents in rural Michoacán where vineyards produced wine for brandy and some red table wine.

"Just like the Italians half a world away," says Victor, "my grandparents made wine." When he was little, "it was common for the kids to have a tequila shot glass of wine with meals. As you grew up the glasses got bigger," he smiles.

The younger of two children, Victor's brother was already in the United States when Victor was a teenager. "All we talked about was the American dream," he recalls. But he wasn't planning on moving north. He had a good job and was in school. Then, in 1980, he visited his brother in Los Angeles. The two took a trip to Potter Valley in eastern Mendocino County for a family wedding. "I liked it better than LA," he says. He also noticed similarities to small agricultural towns in Mexico. He decided it would be a good place to settle, and began networking.

When he was offered a job at a winery overlooking Lake Mendocino, Victor took it. "I had studied English in school and was pretty bilingual when I came here," he says. He knew immediately that being in the winery was what he was meant to do.

Victor was the constant in a winery that changed hands a few times. He worked with different winemakers and did everything from sourcing grapes to making the wines to guiding tours of the winery to sales and marketing. His outgoing personality contributed to his eagerness to learn the business and the respect he has garnered in the industry.

"For nine years, I got exposed to every aspect of the wine industry," he says. Growers asked when he was going to buy their grapes for his own wine. At tastings, consumers asked when was he going to start his own winery.

"Everyone loved my wine and style," he says. In 2004 he, Brenda, and her mother Chris Maine, looked at each other and realized they had all the skills to start a winery. "I always wanted to be in business for myself," says Brenda.

Each Simaine varietal is made from the grapes of a single organically grown vineyard. "I am lucky to know the best vineyards and where to get the organic fruit," says Victor.

He visits the vineyards as they ripen and tastes grapes grown in different blocks. For example, the Zinfandel from Venturi Vineyards in Redwood Valley has a "unique berry flavor" that he likes. He contracts for a whole block, so his wine will have a consistency and reflection of those vines from Venturi's benchland vines. Simaine's Syrah comes from the Tollini vineyard in Calpella. Other Simaine varietals include Sangiovese, Petite Sirah, Merlot and Carignane.

Located in a row of industrial buildings on South State Street in Ukiah, the metal façade of Simaine Cellars is like all the others. Inside, Brenda and her mom have created a cozy tasting room with a window to the barrel room. They decorated the store with display cases of handcrafted gift items,

logo clothing and unique artwork. Brenda's intricate, handcrafted sterling silver jewelry is featured.

At their open houses and holiday events, Victor prepares dishes from his mother country, like pork and chicken verde with warm tortillas to taste with his wines and barrel samples. His philosophy is to marry the vineyard with the cellar and work like his grandparents did. "That means I harvest and make wine for the love of making it."

CESAR TOXQUI CELLARS

MULTI-HERITAGE HEIRLOOMS

Cesar Toxqui (pronounced "ses-zar toe'-ski"), born in Mexico, and Ruth Andres Toxqui, from the Philippines, set in motion their dream to make small quantities of organic food friendly heirloom wine in 2005. By the end of that year, they bottled their first wine Cesar Toxqui Cellars Chardonnay and had red wines aging in barrels.

Cesar Toxqui didn't grow up with wine on the table. He has what he feels is an innate affinity for winemaking that began in Mexico and developed over his last twenty years working in Mendocino wineries.

Cesar grew up near Puebla, one of the first places in Mexico and the New World where the Spaniards planted grapevines in the 1500s. "Wine grapes were all around me and part of my heritage," says Cesar. He moved to the Ukiah at the age of sixteen and, while still in high school, he met the late renowned Mendocino winemaker Jesse Tidwell. "I started on Jess's bottling line, and then I literally moved into the wine world," he says. After graduation from Ukiah High in 1989, he lived with Tidwell and his family for two years.

Cesar helped source grapes and make wine with Tidwell, who started the highly acclaimed former Parsons Creek winery. Later he moved on to a job in the cellar at Brutocao Cellars in Hopland, where he was an assistant to the winemaker.

At the same time, Cesar commuted to Sonoma State University and received his degree in viniculture. He worked harvest and spent time at several local wineries while finishing school. While Cesar was working in wineries, he was also blending homemade wine. He entered some in the Lake County Home Winemakers Festival in Kelseyville. In 2004 and 2005, his wines won the best of show. "People said, 'You should make your own wine.'"

Ruth was nineteen when she came from her native Philippines to Ukiah in 1991 to live with relatives. She had a teaching credential and got a job working in the local schools. Then she got a job at the Department of Motor Vehicles. She and Cesar married in 1995. They have two children, Hugh and Paloma.

As the marketing force for Cesar Toxqui, Ruth knew that in order for her to sell wine she would need to enjoy it. As an excellent cook, she took Cesar's guidance and found their wines to be especially easy to pair with many flavors.

"We are a mom-and-pop boutique winery," says Ruth. "While we know it's hard to break into the business, we love what we do and Cesar is not an armchair winemaker. It's all hands-on at Cesar Toxqui."

In addition to using organically raised grapes, Cesar and Ruth are committed to creating wines that have heritage. Their Heirloom red wine is made from selected Cabernet Sauvignon, Zinfandel and Merlot wines that Cesar blends from every vintage made so far at Cesar Toxqui. Cesar Toxqui Uno Heirloom was released in 2005. Heirloom II was the next vintage and included Pinot Noir.

"It's a unique style," explains Cesar, who plans to continue Heirloom wine until he reaches at least Heirloom X. "Not only are you buying a full-bodied red wine," he says, "but part of our history is in these bottles, each of which contains wine from every vintage we've made so far."

Cesar and Ruth opened a tasting room in Hopland as the first step in their dream of a small roadside cantina or auberge-style destination. "Eventually," says Ruth, "we want to serve Cesar Toxqui wines at a small restaurant with native dishes from our two countries."

ESTERLINA VINEYARDS

DREAMS OF A FATHER

"Dreams of my Father" is not limited to the story of America's forty-fourth President. When it comes to Esterlina Vineyards its founders—an African American family of handsome father and sons and their attractive matriarch—built upon agricultural roots to bring exceptional wine to the market and an esteemed winemaking and grape-growing venture to the wine world.

Esterlina Vineyards' Mendocino winemaking story begins in the 1990s with the purchase of two vineyards. The Sterling family's connection with Mendocino County, however, began in the 1970s.

This was when young people were bailing out of the cities and going "back to the land," getting away from the establishment and living in communes around Mendocino County. Murio and Doris Sterling, already the parents of four sons, were raising cattle on thirty acres in the Central Valley. They were already farmers when they discovered Mendocino.

"Dad always liked to take us on Sunday drives," remembers oldest son Stephen, who is now the marketing manager for Esterlina. On a trip to Potter Valley, they happened on a beautiful 160 acres and next thing Stephen knew, the family was moving. He and his brothers, Eric, Craig and Chris went to Potter Valley Elementary School until Stephen was in the eighth grade.

"Some of our teachers were hippies and lived in VW buses painted with psychedelic designs," says Stephen, adding, "Although my family wasn't like that, we were part of the community and got to know Mendocino during those years."

The boys grew up, followed individual careers, and Murio and Doris moved away. The Sterlings never dreamed they would be working together as a family back in Mendocino County. Twenty years later, Murio and son Eric were out looking at property. They purchased the Cole Ranch, which is known for highly acclaimed Riesling grapes as well as Cabernet Sauvignon and Merlot. And it is America's smallest AVA.

MY GRANDFATHER MADE WINE. SO DID MY DAD. NOT MANY BLACK PEOPLE ARE IN THE WINE BUSINESS, AND THAT'S ANOTHER REASON WHY WE SHOULD BE IN IT.

—MURIO STERLING, ESTERLINA VINEYARDS

Before long, the Sterlings bought the old Pepperwood Springs vineyard on Holmes Ranch Road in Anderson Valley. In 2007, the family added Everett Ridge Winery in Dry Creek Valley in Sonoma County, and that has become Esterlina's winemaking hub.

Everyone has found their place at Esterlina, which translated from Spanish means "Sterling." Craig, an attorney, and Stephen, who has an MBA, manage the winery. Their brother Chris manages the vineyards. Eric is a practicing emergency room doctor in Santa Rosa who is known for his great palate and winemaking skill.

Murio's brother Larry Sterling, a retired electrician, helps with projects at all the properties, which also include vineyard acreage in Sonoma's Alexander Valley and a cattle ranch in the Dominican Republic. Nephew Shon Sterling is the website master. And the next generation including Alex, Andy and Christopher help with harvest and other labor-intensive activities.

When they started out, says Eric, "my parents were not wine drinkers." At their first tastings, Murio garnered attention with his charming southern-style hospitality and when he served Cheetos and chips, not your usual wine fare. "People remembered us."

Murio and Doris often greet visitors at the tasting room. From the deck, all of Anderson Valley stretches out below in one of those views in which the word "breathtaking" is not a trite descriptor. "It's an awesome Pinot Noir site," says Eric.

After years of managing hayfields and cattle, Murio finds grape growing akin to being a gentleman farmer because you don't have to replant every year and the vines will last twenty to thirty years.

He's philosophical about his entry and subsequent success in the wine business. In the beginning, he got to thinking, "Why shouldn't I be in the business? My grandfather made wine. So did my dad. Not many black people are in the wine business, and that's another reason why we should be in it."

LAMB MOWERS,

TURKEYS

AND OTHER
VINEYARD
CRITTERS

Mendocino grape growers, like farmers all over the world, raise animals as well as crops. Most have a family dog or cat. Maple Creek's owners have horses. Parducci's wetlands attract wild birds, ducks and herons. Barra's pond is home to half a dozen geese. Saracina and Navarro use chickens to help keep the bugs out of the vineyards and scratch the dirt. The vineyards at Eaglepoint, McFadden, Nelson and Dempel are adjacent to grazing cattle. The following stories are about a dog becoming a winery name, how tortoises came to a winery, and the benefits of sheep among the vines.

MILANO FAMILY WINERY
HOP KILN AND TORTOISES

CHANCE CREEK
LAMB MOWERS

NAUGHTY BOY
POETRY AND PUPS

MILANO FAMILY
HOP KILN, NURSING AND TORTOISES

Milano Family Winery, located in one of Mendocino's last hop kilns, is the place to see the historic structure and meet Deanna Starr, the vivacious nurse turned winemaker, and her husband Ted, a techie who creates wine business software and loves tortoises—and other animals. You can picnic next to Ted's giant tortoises while tasting Deanna's easy-drinking wines.

"We discovered Hopland on a warm day in May and fell in love with the winery building and Hopland," remembers Deanna. They purchased the seven-acre parcel with the hop kiln and former winery from the Milone family in 2001.

It is one of the last existing hop kilns in Mendocino County and the only one open to the public (tours by appointment). The hop kiln was built in 1947 with all heart redwood. "There's not a knot in the place," says Deanna. As a hop kiln, it was used to dry hops, which are integral to beer making, giving Hopland its name.

As soon as they moved in, Ted redesigned the winery space so Deanna could make wine by herself. "The design of the old building keeps the temperature

perfect," says Deanna. Since it is partially under-ground the temperature stays below seventy degrees even when it's one hundred degrees outside. In the barrel room, once the baling room for the kiln-dried hops, Deanna has 300 oak barrels stacked in rows in different stages of aging. She keeps small metal barrels for her Port and late-harvest wines that don't need the flavor of oak.

Deanna says she finds it fascinating that her nursing skills prepared her for her wine venture. "There's a parallel between nursing and winemaking," she says. It goes like this. A nurse assesses a patient's symptoms. Likewise the winemaker assesses the sugar and acid levels of the grapes. Both create a treatment plan. You have to watch for problems along the way and adjust accordingly. Nursing and winemaking require meticulous cleanliness. And like a patient each grape varietal has its own needs.

As do each of some forty customers for whom Deanna custom crushes. "Making wine for oth-ers is like the doctor coming in with orders," says Deanna, who makes as many as fifty-nine different wines during a harvest season. Some of her clients are growers who make bulk wine and want samples to help sell their grapes. Others choose not to invest in equipment so have their wines made here.

For Milano, Deanna focuses on red wine and dessert wines made from Mendocino County fruit. In addition to her serious Bordeaux-style reds such as Cabernet Sauvignon, Merlot, Petit Verdot and Malbec, Milano produces Zinfandel, Syrah, Carignane, Charbono and Valdiguie. Deanna also makes whites including Chardonnay.

Outside, a grape-covered pergola shades a delightful picnic area. Here the Starrs' love of animals is apparent. A gaggle of Sebastopol geese with ruffled feathers look like they are perpetually molting. Willy Pig is a Vietnamese potbelly who lives with the goats and chickens, including Tina with her showgirl feathered top and strutting walk. A goose sits on a clutch of eggs. Two labs meander among the picnic tables. Sheep and llamas graze on the hillside. Giant tortoises lumber over each other to get to a pile of fresh greens just dumped in their pen.

Ted and Deanna opened a pet store soon after they married in 1993. In 2001, the Starrs bred exotic parrots. At the same time, Ted, who belongs to the Tortoise and Turtle Society, was asked to help take care of giant tortoises when there was a spate of tortoise respiratory problems. Ted learned how to bring them back to health. He and Deanna brought six giant tortoises when they bought the winery.

"We recycle everything and all the animals help out," says Deanna. Enjoying her life as a winemaker and surrounded by her animals she basks in the shadow of the old hop kiln.

CHANCE CREEK
LAMB MOWERS

From late winter to early spring Lou Bock, bundled in a heavy coat and baseball cap, is often seen walking between the dormant rows of Sauvignon Blanc vines surrounded by a flock of sheep. Woolly ewes and a bevy of lambs follow him in anticipation of their next pasture at Chance Creek Vineyard in Redwood Valley.

In June, when the organic grapes begin to ripen, Lou takes the sheep to highlands on a Potter Valley ranch and brings them back after harvest. Classically handsome with a tanned face, his baseball cap covering gray-streaked sandy hair, Lou has an easygoing disposition and gaze that seems to reflect he's not yet where he wants to be. Mostly he's on the road. While he makes about 2000 cases of Chance Creek wine a year, his main job is as a wine distributor.

Since 1981, Lou has commuted almost every weekend between his home near Santa Cruz to Redwood Valley to tend the grapes and keep the equipment running. "I figure I've driven more than a million miles," he says. The vineyard is a passion that necessitates the 500-mile round-trip journey. He splits his time between Redwood Valley, his wine distribution business and his three children.

"I have to sell wine to support my grape-growing habit and keep the farm," he laughs. In 1982, Lou started out representing four small wineries and now has a portfolio of more than thirty wine brands. As his own boss at Bock Wines & Spirits, he was able to spend as much time as possible with his children while they were growing up.

Lou became acquainted with renowned organic gardener Alan Chadwick while attending UC Santa Cruz. In 1979, after a visit with Chadwick, who was farming in Round Valley in eastern Mendocino County, Lou purchased this seventeen-acre property. He milled redwood trees to build his house. He crafted a stone wall behind the wood stove. He roofed with cement tiles to help keep the house cool with no air conditioning.

Lou then planted thirteen acres of Sauvignon Blanc and about two acres of Sangiovese and a little less than an acre of Viognier. He uses the Viognier for blending in both his white Sauvignon Blanc and red Sangiovese and for the Syrah, he makes from grapes grown south of Ukiah. He has noticed that with the addition of Viognier to the Syrah, "all of a sudden the flavor components of both of the grapes are pulled together." It's standard practice in southern France that Viognier is added to the renowned Châteauneuf-du-Pape. "Maybe that's why mine is so good," he quips.

Lou's popular Chance Creek Sauvignon Blanc is made with traditional fermentation and time in oak barrels "coaxing the nuances and roundness with exposure to oak," he explains. He also makes Sauvignon Blanc Terroir 95470, which sees no aging in wood. "I wanted something that was raw, simple and unadulterated to showcase the grape's flavor right from the vineyard," he says.

Lou chose the name Chance Creek to put on his label after reading the book *An Outside Chance* by Thomas McGuane. "McGuane has always drawn me in because his protagonists seem to be trying to repair a cataclysmic malfunction in their lives that is basically rooted in their own perspective as well as the world around them. I often feel like I am in one of McGuane's novels," he says, closing the gate behind the sheep.

"Over the last thirty years farming and running a business I've learned if you want to realize the fruits of your creation it takes time," he says. "Trying to figure out how to coax the best possible flavors out of this land continues to intrigue me." As does keeping the winter weeds down with a flock of sheep.

Naughty Boy Vineyards
Poetry and Pups

Naughty Boy Vineyards is named for a beloved boxer dog named Little Ricky. Subsequent Boxers continue to be part of the story at the Potter Valley vineyard owned by Emjay and Jim Scott.

With a passion for Burgundian-style Pinot Noir and Chardonnay, a circuitous route led the Scotts to create a livelihood growing grapes, making wine and continuing their artistic pursuits.

"To make it work, we both have three jobs," says Emjay, who is also a poet, filmmaker and travel agent. In addition to his long-time employment as a general contractor, Jim designs stylish concrete fireplaces and does the vineyard work himself. They work together selling their wine.

Emjay grew up in Tracy in the California's Central Valley when it was still a farming area. Her dad was a warehouse foreman for Mondavi Winery in Lodi. She went on to get a master's in Video Art from the San Francisco Art Institute and a Masters in Swedish language and literature from the University of California at Berkeley.

Jim, slim with dark brown hair and an understated sense of humor, comes from a salmon fishing family in Victoria, British Columbia, where he grew up. In 1984, he met Emjay while attending the San Francisco Art Institute. Both were in the film program and have continued making short films.

When Emjay and Jim decided they wanted to move to the country they looked at real estate publications distributed in the city. Their first visit to this property in Potter Valley in 1989 intrigued them. It included a hay field, pear orchard and a barn with a cement floor that was used as a cabinetmaker's shop.

In 1990, they bought the property and moved in with their Boxers. They had no idea what they would do. To make ends meet, Emjay taught Swedish and was a substitute teacher. Jim ended up commuting to Marin to work in construction. They sold their house in San Francisco two weeks after the Loma Prieta earthquake.

"We noticed the price of grapes was going up so we got the idea to plant a vineyard," says Emjay. In 1997, the Scotts planted five acres of Pinot Noir. For the next three years, Jim made a little wine at home and began taking winemaking classes at UC

Davis. A friend designed the Naughty Boy label in honor of their dog to put on Jim's homemade wine. At the time, the Scotts sold their grapes to Graziano Family of Wines in Redwood Valley, and then Jim decided to make Naughty Boy wine to sell.

Their first commercial production of Naughty Boy Pinot Noir, made in the Burgundian-style by Jim with Greg Graziano, was released in 2001. Their Naughty Boy Chardonnay is made from grapes grown on Larry Thornton's Potter Valley vineyard. Emjay and Jim have also added the Italian Dolcetto and a dry Rosé of Pinot Noir to their wine list.

Until he died, Naughty Boy's namesake Little Ricky, was Jim's constant companion and is fondly remembered for accompanying Jim into the vineyard at 3:00 a.m. to help with frost protection.

In 2011, Emjay changed her mind about having the words "Naughty Boy" on such a high- quality wine label. While critter labels get mixed professional reviews, Emjay and Jim want to be faithful to their dog. Their newly designed, classy label is simply NBV.

WILD TURKEYS FLOCK INTO THE VINEYARDS JUST BEFORE HARVEST AND HAVE A REPUTATION FOR EATING GRAPES. I TAKE A FIFTY-POUND BAG OF CRACKED CORN AND POUR A THIN TRAIL DOWN THE ROAD AWAY FROM THE VINES. WHEN I GET AS FAR AS I THINK NECESSARY, I DUMP THE REST OF THE BAG INTO A BIG PILE. THE TURKEYS FOLLOW THE TRAIL AND THINK THEY HAVE FOUND THE COOKIE JAR. THEY GORGE THEMSELVES AND HAVE NO ROOM LEFT FOR GRAPES. YOU GOTTA HAVE A LOT OF EXPERIENCE TO OUTSMART A TURKEY.

-CHARLIE BARRA, 85,
MENDOCINO'S "DEAN" OF WINEGROWERS

BORDEAUX
IN MENDO

Passion for the wines of Bordeaux, one of France's most historic, celebrated and legendary wine regions, inspire the winemakers in this section. Only six major red grape varietals—Cabernet Sauvignon, Merlot, Petite Verdot, Cabernet Franc, Malbec and Carménère—may be used in a blend labeled "Bordeaux." Two whites—Sauvignon Blanc and Semillon—are typical. Mendocino's Bordeaux lovers found compatible sites to grow wines they would put up against the best in the world. In addition to the four featured here, many more wineries in Mendocino County, from Philo to Hopland and Potter Valley to Ukiah, produce Cabernet Sauvignon, Merlot and Sauvignon Blanc. Among others who specialize in a Bordeaux varietal are Oster, McNab Ridge, Milano and Terra Sávia.

YORKVILLE CELLARS
ORGANICALLY BORDEAUX

DUNCAN PEAK
HISTORIC SITE REFLECTED IN HANDCRAFTED WINE

ROSATI FAMILY WINERY
CABERNET ON THE RUSSIAN RIVER

COLE BAILEY VINEYARDS
SESQUIPEDALIAN

VIEW OF DUNCAN PEAK FROM THE VALLEY

YORKVILLE CELLARS

ORGANICALLY BORDEAUX

When Yorkville Cellars' owners Deborah and Edward Wallo purchased 110 acres with a small vineyard in 1988, they began a lifestyle different from their international world of marketing and Internet development.

"We didn't set out to be in the wine business," says Edward, looking back over more than two decades of certified organic grape growing and the most awards for any wine using organically raised grapes. "We were looking for a great place to raise our three kids."

Edward and Deborah both grew up in the country. He was raised in Oregon, she near Wales in Great Britain. Both led high-powered professional lives, learned to love wine and had the opportunity to live in some of the world's best wine regions. In the 1980s, he was in international marketing and she was an attorney. They met on a weekend visit with mutual friends in Wales. They married in 1987 and

lived in German and Italian wine country, before a stint in Paris with weekend treks to Bordeaux.

In the late 1980s, after moving back to the United States and living in Silicon Valley, they were drawn to Mendocino County by a magazine article. "The next weekend we started looking for property," says Edward. "We liked the idea of having land and possibly a vineyard."

When they saw this property, with a small Sauvignon Blanc vineyard, and met some of the neighbors, they were hooked. Their acreage rises from 1,000 to 1,200-foot elevation. Neighboring hills are ringed with conifers, reminding Edward of his native Oregon. A geographical distinction, denoted by a row of poplar trees, is the dividing line between the drainage to the Russian River on the south and the Navarro River basin on the north.

At first, the Wallos sold the grapes, but they kept seeing the wines made from their grapes winning medals, so in 1989 and 1990 they tripled the vineyard acreage.

"We had the idea to plant Bordeaux varietals and make a blend, as families have done for generations in France," says Edward. They planted Semillon next to the Sauvignon Blanc. Each year the Wallos hope these grapes will get to the ripe raisiny stage to become a late-harvest wine like Bordeaux's famed late-harvest Sauternes. The secret to making this style of late harvest is a particular unpredictable fungus known as *Botrytis cinerea* or the "noble rot," which settles into the grape during the right wet, then warm, conditions.

In addition to the white varietals terraced up the hill, the Wallos planted all six of the "noble red grapes" that come from the renowned Bordeaux wine region: Cabernet Sauvignon, Merlot, Cabernet Franc, Carménère, Malbec and Petit Verdot.

"Given how long it takes for vines to mature and then adding barrel aging, it took about eight years before we finally got to taste the wine," says Edward. Mendocino's renowned winemaker Greg Graziano joined as winemaker in 1995, and he and the Wallos produce Yorkville Cellars' wines.

The Wallos named their Bordeaux-style red blend Richard the Lionheart, and the white Eleanor of Aquitaine. They also bottle each of the five Bordeaux varietals separately and offer tastings for each varietal, which is a rare experience in the wine country. While Cabernet Sauvignon and Merlot are popular

in many places, having the opportunity to taste the nuances and differences of the other Bordeaux varietals is an education. "They are like children in a family," explains Edward. "Each is similar but distinct and when blended their synergy affects the outcome we are looking for in our wine."

The driveway to the hillside red barnwood tasting room is lined with 500 rose bushes along the vineyard rows. It is furnished with French and British antiques and stocked with locally artisan-made crafts. Every window has a view of the organic vineyards. Three magnificent ancient oaks around the building shade the deck where picnickers taste the blends and Yorkville's varietals.

Deborah and Edward are usually around Yorkville Cellars, working in the vineyards, on marketing or sales and pouring tastes. "It was serendipitous that we ended up here," says Deborah.

Duncan Peak
Site Reflected in Handcrafted Wine

"Our mission is to make excellent wines for people to enjoy, and to preserve this property exactly the way we found it," says Hubert Lenczowski. He and his wife, Resa are proprietors of Duncan Peak Vineyards on Mountain House Road just west of Hopland.

Their 110-acre property was part of the 15,000-acre Rancho Sanel Mexican land grant awarded to Fernando Feliz in the early 1800s. In 1858, Elijah Duncan built the barn from virgin redwood planks and timber. Duncan's name lives on not only on this wine label but also on the 2,450-foot peak that rises to the west.

Hubert's parents bought the ranch in 1962, and he has been coming here since he was six years old and he grew up on these rolling hills near Feliz Creek. When he and Resa married in 1982, they bought the ranch from his family.

"I had a dream of doing something agricultural on the property," says Hubert. "Some of our neighbors, like the Fetzers, Jim Milone and Bill Crawford, were growing grapes and making great wine, so it made sense to plant a vineyard." He planted one acre of Cabernet Sauvignon. Repeating his family

tradition, Hubert and Resa and their two children spent weekends and summers in Hopland.

Since the early 1980s, the Lenczowskis have added ten acres of Cabernet Sauvignon and one acre of Petite Sirah. Their first vintage of Cabernet was pressed in 1986 and released in 1989.

Over the years, Hubert and Resa have refurbished the old buildings, reusing the original square nails that were used to build the barn when he remodeled it into a winery. The cow stalls were refit to hold winery equipment. A hipped shed, which was once for sheep and chickens, is now a temperature-controlled cellar for barrel aging.

The small scale of the vineyard and winery means Hubert can do everything by hand. While not paper certified, everything at Duncan Peak is organic. When the grapes start to turn from green to purple, the process known as veraison, Hubert cuts clusters of berries off the vines. "We leave one or two bunches per cane."

Some years, an acre only produces one ton of grapes. "That's great news for a winemaker like me," he says. It seems there is an inverse relationship between quality and quantity. "The less you have the better. That's because the vigor from the vines goes into the smaller crop of grape clusters, just like the Grand Crus of Bordeaux in France." he explains.

Duncan Peak wines are drinkable soon after they are bottled and they are ageworthy. That's because the Cabernet and Petite Sirah are not super high alcohol and tannic. "I've tried fancy cult wines that at ten years old are not ready to drink, and the fruit is already dead," he explains. "Ours at ten and fifteen years are still vibrant and fruit rich. You don't need to have a lot of tannins and alcohol to have a long-lasting wine."

The Lenczowskis' home at Duncan Peak vineyards is a bungalow built by Bessie Duncan in 1945 out of materials from the original Duncan Victorian. It perches on a knoll shaded by trees and with just enough room on the small plateau for a lawn and a porch from which to sip Cabernet and watch the sun set over Duncan Peak.

"Our story is of authenticity," says Hubert. "Wine made on this property is a reflection of what these soils and this place can produce."

ROSATI FAMILY WINERY

CABERNET ON THE RUSSIAN RIVER

When Mario Rosati purchased an old cattle ranch south of Hopland in 1980, he never dreamed he would be in the wine business. However, in 1987, when he was given bud wood from one of the world's most renowned Cabernet Sauvignon vineyards, he planted his own small vineyard.

Like a brilliant green tiara, the Rosati vineyard crowns the golden oak-studded hills at 1,000 feet above the Russian River south of Hopland on one of Mendocino County's heritage ranches. The Cabernet Sauvignon bud wood originated from Ridge Vineyard's Monte Bello vineyard in the Santa Cruz Mountains.

Mario, a corporate attorney, loves to tell how he came to grow grapes related to the prestigious Ridge Vineyards. In 1971, John Wilson, a senior partner at his law firm, asked Mario to take on a

new client. "John was a Scotch drinker and knew that I preferred wine," says Mario, who started as the corporate attorney for Ridge Vineyards and later served on the winery's board of directors.

Ridge's claim to fame came in 1976 when their 1971 Cabernet Sauvignon was entered in the "Judgment of Paris tasting" (the subject of the movie *Bottle Shock*). Ridge ranked fifth in this first international tasting pitting five French Bordeaux wines against five California Cabernets. Thirty years later, at a re-tasting of the same wines, the 1971 Ridge came in first.

In the beginning, Mario and his wife, Danelle Storm Rosati, made wine from their estate-grown Rosati Cabernet vineyard for their family, friends and charities. The two native Californians and longtime aficionados of great wine traveled distinctive paths on their way to becoming wine producers. Mario grew up in the East Bay in a close-knit Italian family and Danelle in the central valley and in Santa Barbara.

A graduate of UCLA and Boalt Law School, Mario has been an attorney with the same Palo Alto-based law firm for forty years.

Danelle discovered wine while living abroad for several years, initially during her junior year in Madrid, Spain. Upon returning to California in 1978, she started her own executive search firm specializing in high-tech and life-science industries.

Danelle and Mario met in 1991. One year later, the Rosati vineyard was producing enough grapes to bottle the first vintage. Danelle suggested that they design a label for the bottle. "We produced 200 cases and the family came together to work on the design," she says. Today the family includes three daughters (all attorneys, Mario is proud to say), and three grandchildren.

In addition to producing and marketing Rosati Family Cabernet Sauvignon, the two Rosatis still work more than full-time professions. "We spend much of our free time 'doing wine,'" says Danelle. They also entertain frequently at their ranch where they remodeled the once ramshackle 150-year-old farmhouse and the hundred-year-old barn.

"Our winery is not a business; it's a passion," says Mario, who also loves to fly planes, scuba dive and hunt. His father, Guido, used to say, "Mario likes to tickle the tail of the dragon."

"We love fine wine and food," they both say. Danelle has created two small cookbooks with a third in the making. They include beef, lamb, fish and appetizer recipes from some of the renowned chefs from such restaurants as Square One, Evvia, Marche, Bistro Elan, Pebble Beach Resort's Peppoli, and Mendocino's own Café Beaujolais.

"Our Old World-style wines pair well with a variety of foods," says Danelle. She describes Rosati wines as fruit forward, elegant and balanced. "They express the best of their own very special vines."

COLE BAILEY VINEYARDS
SESQUIPEDALIAN

"We felt the climate on the hillsides in inland Mendocino County could grow excellent Cabernet Sauvignon," say Bob Anderson and Jennifer Malloy of Cole Bailey Vineyards. They named their wine Sesquipedalian.

It might seem that a winery that uses a name spoofing the use of long pompous words isn't serious. When you learn that one of the winery's owners was the prototype for the character Otter in the movie classic *Animal House*, you might think the winery is quirky.

While both the wine name and the *Animal House* reference are true about Redwood Valley's Cole Bailey Vineyards, it's doubtful you'll find a couple more seriously committed to winemaking excellence. Bob Anderson and Jennifer Malloy produce two wines: Sesquipedalian Bordeaux-style red and a crisp fruity Sauvignon Blanc.

The dictionary says sesquipedalian refers to long and ponderous words. Cole Bailey on their website defines it as "a sophistical rhetorician inebriated with the exuberance of his own verbosity." Jennifer and Bob wanted their wine not to be intimidating and snotty.

"Our silly label is intended to encourage people to learn about wine," says Jennifer. Their sense of humor continues on their website, which lists what they call the "world's worst wine words" and invites bloggers to join in with their own.

Both Jennifer and Bob are practicing attorneys to "help pay for the wine habit." Their vineyard moniker comes from their son's name, Cole, and a family name Bailey. Bob is managing partner at Santa Rosa's largest law firm. Jennifer is general counsel to an education company.

When Bob was at Dartmouth College, he was a fraternity buddy of Chris Miller, who wrote the screenplay for the movie *Animal House*. "The reason the movie is still popular today is that it reminds everyone of their college experience," says Bob, who was known as "Otter" in his fraternity. *Animal House* became a hit. Bob became an attorney.

In the early 1980s, Bob was one of the founders of Mount Konocti Winery in Lake County. It was later sold to Jed Steele. When he and Jennifer saw this hillside setting with a vineyard in 2001, they fell in love with it, says Jennifer. The property is terraced up the south-facing hill at the north end of Redwood Valley. A lovely redwood-sided home with its green metal roof sits on the widest terrace. Stone patios and a swimming pool are shaded with tall evergreens and some oak trees. A charming wine cellar is situated into the hillside next to the pool. There were 500 Syrah and Sangiovese vines when they bought it.

They've replanted with Bordeaux varietals—Cabernet Sauvignon, Petite Verdot, Cabernet Franc, Malbec and Merlot—in proportion to their blend, of which 85 percent is Cabernet. The grapes grow on terraces wide enough to allow a small tractor to pass by.

Cole Bailey's goal is to make elegant, European-style wine. "We want to make the best wine we can," says Anderson, "not try to make wine just to get a score from a certain critic." They also make a little Syrah with the label Otter's Road Trip Red.

You don't have to pronounce Sesquipedalian to get the joke. It's Malloy and Anderson's way of saying, "We want to be inclusive."

MENDOCINO
DREAMIN'

Mendo-euphoria is a term local realtors use for the feeling that first draws a newcomer who can't resist settling in this ruggedly beautiful county. There are many stories about people seduced by Mendocino possibilities and every story in this book could fit under this title. This section offers a sampling of the variety of ways the draw to Mendocino permeates and succeeds.

BINK WINES
BIG DREAMS

LULA CELLARS
LIVING THE DREAM

BREGGO CELLARS
LOCAL GRAPES AND ACCOLADES

MacGREGOR'S TRINAFOUR CELLAR
MENDO WINES WITH SCOTTISH FLAIR

DENNIS MARTIN, DIRECTOR OF WINEMAKING, FETZER

BINK WINES

BIG DREAMS

Two miles up a gravel mountain road northwest of Yorkville, a magnificent Douglas fir tree shades a couple of lawn chairs. Hawk's Butte rises to a peak in the background. Seven acres of Merlot and Syrah vines encircle a pond and green the golden hillside in the summer.

The idyllic setting is the home of Bink Vineyards where the motto "Dream Big, Act Now, Love Life" written on the homepage of their website is the modus operandi of owners Deborah Schatzlein, winemaker, and Cindy Paulson, winegrower.

Schatzlein and Paulson both worked for an environmental engineering company in Boulder, Colorado, for more than twenty years. Paulson is a fourth-generation Californian who grew up in Washington, when her dad moved the family to farm table grapes, peaches and asparagus.

Deborah and Cindy bought the forty-acre property known as Hawk's Butte in Yorkville Highlands in 1998. In 2001, Schatzlein left her job and Paulson transferred to the Walnut Creek headquarters of their company.

Cindy kept her day job "so we can buy things like French oak barrels." In her spare time Cindy takes care of their vineyard along with fifteen fruit trees. "We also have a good experienced vineyard manager," adds Deborah.

Describing her transition from environmental engineer to winemaker, Deborah says, "It was surreal in hindsight." From the beginning she immersed herself in winemaking, took classes at UC Davis and apprenticed with respected winemaker Jill Davis, doing everything from harvest to lab work and cellar jobs. She then spent three years at a small winery in Yountville.

With degrees in chemistry and biology, Deborah knows her way around a lab. "You don't just depend on a number for good wine," she explains, "you have to make sure there are no bad microbes. The rest is sensory evaluation. "I have to use my nose and my intuition."

Both Cindy and Deborah connect their environmental expertise with their winegrowing and winemaking. "We think carefully about how we farm, it has to be sustainable," says Cindy, noting that their steep sloping site is challenging. "Farming is science and art, but you also have to have a sense of humor," she says.

Wondering about the name Bink? Cindy and Deborah really like Syrah, which is why they planted it at Hawk's Butte. "Black ink" is an industry nickname for Syrah, which they shortened to Bink. When Bink's 2006 Syrah was chosen as one of the top one hundred wines by *Wine Enthusiast* magazine, they felt the name was justified. Deborah also makes Sauvignon Blanc, which she calls "the red wine drinkers' white wine." In addition Bink produces Lumineaux, a rosé of their estate Merlot, Pinot Noir, Merlot and Melange, a blend of Merlot and Cabernet Sauvignon.

Living their motto, Cindy and Deborah are often found at Bink's tasting room in the Mediterranean villa just south of Philo on Highway 128 in Anderson Valley. "It's been quite a ride, a lot of hard work," says Deborah. Cindy agrees and adds, "It's worth it."

LULA
CELLARS
LIVING THE
DREAM

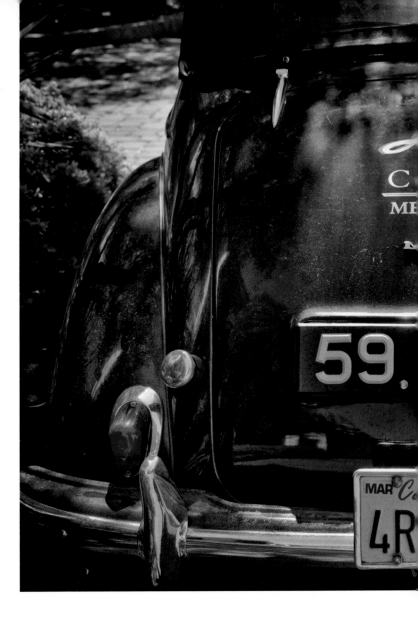

In 2002, when Jeff Hansen discovered a vineyard that produces extraordinary Pinot Noir grapes a dozen miles from the Mendocino Coast, he decided it was time to realize a long-held dream.

"I was looking for a place to make wine. I wanted to drink and sell it directly through a tasting room," says Jeff, winemaker-proprietor of Lula Cellars. His tasting room is located in the Mediterranean villa on Highway 128 six miles northwest of Boonville in Anderson Valley. After working fourteen years as a commercial product photographer in southern California, Jeff decided, "Life is only so long." A longtime wine aficionado, he decided to move to Northern California for a slower pace. He landed a job working at a vineyard and winery in Napa Valley. For the next seven years, Jeff immersed himself into learning every part of the industry from grape growing to winemaking to sales.

During those years, he visited vineyards around northern California, including in Mendocino County where he especially loved to spend time on the coast. In 2002, Hansen came upon Joe Harris's Costa Vineyard in Comptche. Wanting to do something on a smaller scale, Hansen started producing Pinot Noir from Harris's vineyard and

his winery Lula after his maternal grandmother, who was born in 1879 in the Oklahoma Territory. He wanted to honor Lula because "she taught me about never losing faith when all seems lost."

Hansen opened Lula Cellars in 2010 in the villa that was built as a home and business complex.

"Although the exterior is very Mediterranean, I wanted inside to reflect Mendocino-style," says Jeff. Local carpenter Gary Poehlman built the tasting bar from redwood that grew in Anderson Valley. A handcrafted barnwood "Mendocino" sign hangs on the tasting room's mottled golden-hued walls.

In the warm weather tables and chairs are set up in the courtyard. Lula wines are available for sale by the glass or the bottle for those who want to picnic. Two other Mendocino winery tasting rooms are in the complex, Drew and Bink. Upstairs are beautifully appointed vacation rental suites called The Madrones. "We want this to be a destination," says Jeff.

In addition to Lula's full-bodied, critically acclaimed Pinot Noir, Jeff makes dry Gewurztraminer, old vine Zinfandel and Rosato, a dry rosé that is half Zinfandel and half Pinot Noir.

Jeff drives from his home in the village of Mendocino to the tasting room four days a week. "Then I go home and see the sunset over the ocean," he smiles. As the advertising photographer turned winemaker puts it, "Where you start and where you end up is sometimes a surprise."

also from another Comptche vineyard owned by John Peterson.

Jeff was aware that making wine from Pinot Noir grapes is not the easiest way to go into winemaking. "Even though it is the hardest grape to grow and make into wine, I love it," he says.

"From the first wine I made from those Comptche grapes, I was realizing my dream," says Jeff. He named

BREGGO CELLARS

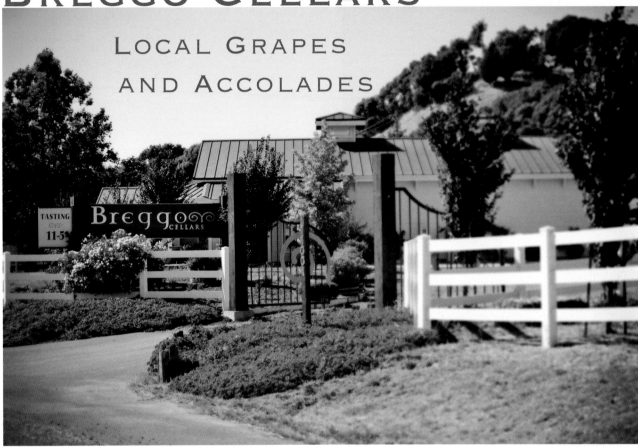

LOCAL GRAPES
AND ACCOLADES

Breggo Cellars is located in the 1920s yellow craftsman farmhouse just north of Boonville on Highway 128. The property, an old sheep ranch, was named Breggo, the word for "sheep" in Boontling, the folk language created in Anderson Valley a hundred years ago.

Breggo's label has a hand-drawn ram, whose curved horns are mimicked on the entry gate. Using old-fashioned techniques, such as limited intervention in winemaking, and incorporating what is state-of-the-art in viticulture, Breggo Cellars has rocketed to acclaim since its first wine was released in 2004.

Breggo uses all Anderson Valley grapes sourced from such vineyards as Donnelly Creek, Ferrington, Wiley, Alder Springs and Savoy. A frictionless French grape press bestows a gentle pressing of the grapes.

Since 2009, when Breggo was purchased by Napa Valley vintner Cliff Lede, Ryan Hodgins has been the winemaker. Particularly fond of Anderson Valley's Pinot Gris with its peach-pear aromas and Pinot Noir's dense cherry ripeness, especially from the grapes at Savoy Vineyards, Ryan is continuing Breggo's reputation for great tasting wines.

Breggo's founder Doug Stewart designed the vineyard so the vines are evenly spaced and the watering lines are underground. A mower can go in either direction to keep weeds down. With the water source underneath the vines, weeds don't grow as readily and there is less worry about mildew in this cool coastal valley where the fog slips in during the ripening season. "And we still have a billion frogs in the vineyard," says Stewart.

Of their five varietals, Breggo's Pinot Noir, Chardonnay and Syrah are unfiltered. Ryan continues to use the best Anderson Valley grapes and minimal intervention. The result is repeated high acclaim associated with Anderson Valley Pinot Noir and to Breggo wines. Breggo was awarded the best new winery in 2008 by *Food & Wine* magazine. Other Breggo varietals include Pinot Gris, Chardonnay, Syrah, Riesling, Gewurztraminer and Rosé of Syrah.

Inside the tasting room, the knowledgeable staff guides you through a tasting at the easy-to-mosey-up cherry-wood bar with a redwood kickboard. Floor-to-ceiling French doors open to a picnic area between the tasting room and Highway 128. Another set of French doors allows a view to the cellar where French and Hungarian oak barrels are stacked, a bottling machine is tucked into a corner, and humidifiers prevent evaporation. A gas stove in the corner is ready to warm up winter tastings.

MacGregor's
Trinafour Cellars
Mendo Wines with Scottish Flair

Paying homage to his Scottish ancestry, Alex MacGregor launched Trinafour Cellars in 2005. Alex, who grew up in Toronto, Canada, is the full-time winemaker at Saracina Vineyards north of Hopland. His father, Ian MacGregor, was born in the hamlet of Trinafour in Scotland. The senior MacGregor appreciated fine wine and had a wine collection, but "my only claim to an agricultural background harkens to my great-grandfather who was the gamekeeper at an estate in Trinafour," says Alex.

In 1985, Alex received a degree in international marketing and finance at McGill University and worked part-time in a restaurant. "After traveling

for a year in France and Spain, I got interested in wine," he says. Upon his return to Toronto, he used his newfound interest to work on wine lists in the high-end restaurants where he was employed.

"As the person in charge of the wine list, I got to buy and taste of a lot of great wines," he recalls. The emphasis at one establishment was on Rhône wines from the south of France. "I got a good education in really good French peasant wines," he says.

Alex was accepted to California State University at Fresno, where he crammed every enology class they offered into three semesters. He moved to Sonoma

County, received a degree in viticulture at Santa Rosa Community College and looked up one of the contacts he made while working in Toronto.

"I started as a harvest intern and lab rat at Dry Creek Vineyards," he says. For the next few years, he had the opportunity to work with some of the industry's best winemakers.

In 1994, MacGregor met Kathleen and they got married. Their first son, Ian, was born in 1997, "one of the great port years," says MacGregor. Second son, Duncan, was born in 2000, "another phenomenal port year." Needless to say he put down some of those vintage ports to celebrate future milestones.

In 2002, Alex was looking for a change and John Fetzer was launching Saracina Winery. Alex got the job as winemaker and the MacGregors moved to Ukiah.

When Alex had an opportunity to visit Alvin Tollini's Niemi Vineyard in Redwood Valley, he was inspired by the fifty-to-sixty-year old Carignane vines, dry-farmed and organic "by default."

"The story of Carignane is untapped," he says. In the early years of California viticulture Carignane was the most widely planted grape and was used from the 1940s until the 1960s to make the blends known as "burgundy" before varietal grapes became popular.

Alex is drawn to Carignane's peasant qualities, reminiscent of the French country wines. "It's not a sexy variety," he says. The Carignane and the Petite

Sirah he uses for his wines were both planted by Tollini's Niemi Vineyard's namesake.

Alex also makes a dry white wine from Muscat Canelli, usually known as a sweet wine. He calls this style of Muscat Canelli "Italy meets Alsace," because it is dry yet has the aromatic qualities typical of Muscat Canelli.

Alex is enamored with the historical aspect as well as the potential for producing elegant Mendocino wines that are easy to drink. Trinafour's Petite Sirah is characteristically deep purple. Its flavor is round and fruity, spicy and smooth and goes remarkably well with a range of dishes.

Of equal importance is Alex's Scottish ancestry. Trinafour labels include an eye-catching red and blue family tartan and recognition of MacGregor's ancestral home in Perthshire, Scotland.

ONLY IN MENDOCINO

CORO REPRESENTS A REPUTATIONAL
ROLL OF THE DICE THAT FEW WINE
REGIONS HAVE MADE.

—THOM ELKJER,
SAN FRANCISCO CHRONICLE
JUNE 10, 2004

CORO MENDOCINO

PROTOCOL AND HERITAGE

EACH BLEND IS DIFFERENT—ALTHOUGH ZIN DOMINATES—AND, HAVING TASTED THROUGH THEM ALL, I CAN VOUCH FOR THEIR QUALITY.

—JEFF COX, *PRESS DEMOCRAT*
FEBRUARY 12, 2011

In 2001, a group of Mendocino winemakers challenged themselves to create a wine derived from Mendocino's wine heritage, individual diversity and best grape varietals. These veteran winemakers, including Paul Dolan, Dennis Patton, Fred Nickel, Greg Graziano, and Casey Hartlip, created Coro Mendocino.

"Coro means chorus in Italian," says third generation winemaker Greg Graziano of Graziano Family of Wines in Redwood Valley. He represents one of a dozen or so wineries that produce their version of Coro Mendocino.

Each winemaker follows the unique Coro Consortium Production Protocol, which requires that the wine is made in accordance with a prescribed set of standards inspired by such legendary European wine designations as France's Châteauneuf-du-Pape and Italy's Chianti Classico. In addition, Coro Mendocino raises the bar with periodic structured peer reviews and blind tastings to ensure all wines are made to those exacting quality standards before they are bottled and labeled.

The tasting and reviews take place over the three years from grape juice to bottle release. Fellow winemakers evaluate each wine in order to reach the quality and flavor profile Coro is known for. "The tastings are brutal," says Guinness McFadden of McFadden Vineyards in Potter Valley.

The common varietal in every Coro Mendocino wine is Zinfandel, which can be as little as 40 percent or as much as 70 percent. "One of the best wines in Mendocino County is Zinfandel. It has history and quality and a lot of wines blend well with it," says Graziano. His Coro is 56 percent Zinfandel.

In addition to some Petite Sirah, he blends in Barbera, Dolcetto and Sangiovese giving a salute to his Italian heritage.

Individual winemakers determine other varietals added to the Coro blend. McFadden's 2006 Coro is a blend of Zinfandel plus Petite Sirah and Syrah.

"Each Coro wine has a 'house palate' that distinguishes it," says Patton. The two Coro wines he has made have similar blends of about half Zinfandel and the other half fairly evenly split between Syrah and Petite Sirah. The flavors, however, exhibit subtle differences that evoke the terroir of their vineyards.

"Coro is perfectly suited to me," says Sally Ottoson, winemaker at Pacific Star. She makes wine from grown in as many as fifteen different vineyards all over Mendocino County. She looks for balance in her blend. She'll add Charbono because it's "age-worthy," Petite Sirah for color and body, and Pinot Noir for an elegant "perfume" at the end.

"It's fun to try different combinations," says David Brutocao of Brutocao Cellars. "Most of Brutocao's wines are one hundred percent varietals," he explains, "but we grow a lot of different grapes and this is a chance to combine the best of what we like." Brutocao's 2006 Coro combines Barbera, Syrah and Dolcetto with 60 Zinfandel.

Another lover of blending wines is Heather McKelvey, of Philo Ridge. "I am inspired by Côtes du Rhône blends and, like a chef, I like to play with different flavors." Her blend includes such Rhône varietals as Syrah and Petite Syrah along with a dose of Carignane.

"There is no other wine designation in the world made like Coro," says Dennis Patton, who has been making wine in Mendocino County for thirty years. He makes Coro Mendocino for Golden Vineyards. "When we sit down for tastings we can vote a wine out if it isn't good enough. That can't happen anywhere else in the world."

MENDOCINO

WINE FESTIVALS, EVENTS, WINE CLUBS, AND RESOURCES

When the wineries open for their showcase events on weekends throughout the year, it's a perfect time to delve into the best of what Mendocino wine country is all about. Visit winery websites to find out when their next events are.

In addition to the wineries, monthly and weekly events are happening at Sip! Mendocino, Patrona Restaurant in Ukiah, Enoteca Bar in Ukiah, the Wine Bar(n) at Glendeven, and the Mendocino Hotel.

Check the Visit Mendocino, complete website at visitmendocino.com or mendowine.com to find more details and other events.

On the following pages are major events in Mendocino County, listed by season.

JANUARY

Mendocino County Crab, Wine & Beer Festival
www.visitmendocino.com

FEBRUARY

Anderson Valley International Alsatian Varietals Festival
www.avwines.com

In Love With Redwood Valley
www.atasteofredwoodvalley.com

MARCH

Mendocino Coast Whale Festivals
Mendocino, Little River, Ft. Bragg
www.mendocinocoast.com

APRIL

Where the Earth IS First Festival
www.visitmendocino.com

Whale and Jazz Festival - South Coast
www.redwoodcoastchamber.com

MAY

Hopland Passport - Spring
www.hoplandpassport.com

Anderson Valley Pinot Noir Festival
www.avwines.com

Boonville Beer Festival
www.avbc.com

Willits Community Festival & Car Show
www.willits.org

JUNE

A Taste of Redwood Valley
Father's Day Weekend
www.atasteofredwoodvalley.com

A Taste of Mendocino - in San Francisco
www.tasteofmendocino.com

Sierra Nevada World Music Festival - Boonville
www.snwmf.com

JULY

World's Largest Salmon BBQ
www.salmonrestoration.com

Willits Frontier Days
www.willitsfrontierdays.com

Mendocino Music Festival
www.mendocinomusic.com

AUGUST

Redwood Empire Fair
www.redwoodempirefair.com

Mendocino County Wine Competition
www.mendocinowinecompetition.com

SEPTEMBER

Paul Bunyan Days - Fort Bragg
www.paulbunyandays.com

**Willits Kinetic Carnivale &
Roots of Motive Power Steam Festival**
www.kineticcarnivale.com
www.rootsofmotivepower.com

Winesong!
www.winesong.org

Mendocino County Fair and Apple Show
www.mendocinocountyfair.com

OCTOBER

Ukiah Country Pumpkinfest
www.cityofukiah.com

**World'sChampionship Abalone
Cookoff & Festival**
www.mendoparks.org

Willits Harvest Moon Celebration
www.willits.org

Hopland Passport - Fall
www.hoplandpassport.com

NOVEMBER

**Mendocino Beer, Wine &
Mushroom Festival**
www.visitmendocino.com

**Holiday Wine Sale and Juried
Artisan Faire** - Redwood Valley
www.atasteofredwoodvalley.com

DECEMBER

Mendocino Coast Candlelight Inn Tour
www.mendocinoinntour.com

Festival of Lights - Fort Bragg
www.gardenbythesea.org

Holiday Express - Willits
www.rootsofmotivepower.com
www.mendocinomuseum.org

WINE CLUBS

Nearly every winery in Mendocino County has a wine club. Joining is free. Signing up means you agree to a certain number of shipments within a price range for the year. The membership continues until you opt to end it. Prices range from $40 a shipment to around $100 and you can choose your level when you sign up. The wine is shipped two to twelve times a year. Charges are automatically made to credit cards at the time of shipments. You can sign up at the winery or on their website.

In addition to making wine shipments, each winery offers special discounts, invitations to private tastings, tickets to public tastings, and at least one annual event just for the members. The themes of these events are as varied as the wineries and their owners. They have included a poker party, hoedown, the tropics, circus, grape stomp, winemaking fantasy camp, blending and tasting competitions, ladybug release, and pig roast. Some wineries have "pick-up" parties, if you choose to pick up your wine rather than have it shipped.

If a winery has a tasting charge in the tasting room, it is usually waived for club members, who also have special tasting and touring privileges. Wine club members receive new releases, which is especially advantageous at small wineries that sell out quickly. Some wineries offer discounts to a guest house or other lodging facility.

Some wine clubs also offer discounts for merchandise sold in the tasting room. Everything from logo hats and shirts to local food products, books, tableware, pottery, handcrafts and jewelry are found in winery tasting rooms, which makes them one of the best places to shop for a unique and often locally-made gift.

Resources

✿ **Anderson Valley Winegrowers Association**

(AVWA)   www.avwines.com

✿ **Anderson Valley Chamber of Commerce**

www.andersonvalleychamber.com

(707) 895–2379

✿ **Destination Hopland**

www.destinationhopland.com

✿ **Hopland Passport**

www.hoplandpassport.com

 (800) 564–2582

✿ **Mendocino Coast Chamber of Commerce**

www.mendocinocoast.com

(707) 961–6300

✿ **Mendocino County Museum and Wine History Project**

www.MendocinoMuseum.org

 (707) 459–2736

✿ **Mendo Limos**

www.mendocinowinetours.com

(707) 964–8294; (707) 964-3509

✿ **Mendocino Wine Tours**

www.mendowinetours.com

 (707) 937–6700; (888) 805–TOUR (8687)

✿ **Redwood Coast Chamber of Commerce**

www.redwoodcoastchamber.com

(800) 778–5252; (707) 884–1080

✿ **Sip! Mendocino Tasting Room & Wine Shop**

www.sipmendocino.com

(707) 744–8375

✿ **Skunk Train**

www.skunktrain.org

(866) 457–5865

✿ **A Taste of Redwood Valley**

www.atasteofredwoodvalley.com

(707) 485–0322

✿ **Tour Mendocino Wines**

www.tourmendocinowines.com

 (707) 849–2700

✿ **Ukiah Greater Valley Chamber of Commerce**

www.ukiahchamber.com

(707) 462-4705

✿ **Visit Mendocino County**

www.visitmendocino.com

 (866) 466-3636

✿ **Willits Chamber of Commerce**

www.willits.org

(707) 459–7100

MENDOCINO
WINE ROUTES
AND WINERIES

Mendocino County's three major wine touring routes meander along river canyons, next to coastal bluffs, over narrow ridges, across big and small valleys, through agricultural heartland, and into small towns. They follow the major highways in Mendocino County: US Highway 101, also known as the Redwood Highway; State Route 128, California's "Wine Road," and California State Route 1, the Pacific Coast Highway.

Along the way, you'll experience a relaxed pace while viewing vineyards, lavender fields, sunflower patches, and olive, pear and apple orchards, as well as magnificent redwood and fir groves, and ever dramatic ocean vistas. Seasonally changing vineyards, orchards, roadside fruit and vegetable stands, and farmers' markets dot the way.

Livestock ranching is making a comeback and farmers' markets throughout the county offer locally raised beef, pork, goat, lamb and chickens, as well as cheese, honey, jam, olive oil, vinegar, herbs, and salt.

Here is a preview of what you will find on each of Mendocino's wine routes. For more touring details, and information on museums, galleries, art centers, lodging, dining, and more things to do besides wine tasting, Visit Mendocino's website and visitor publications offer up-to-date listings and contacts around the county.

Each of Mendocino's wineries is listed alphabetically, according to area, with the website and telephone number. Those that are profiled in this book are in BOLD.

Highway 128:

Yorkville Highlands and Anderson Valley

Highway 128 is Mendocino County's fifty-eight-mile link between the coast and the rest of the world. From Highway 101, Highway 128 heads up the Dry Creek Watershed and down the Navarro River watershed to the Pacific Ocean. Sheep ranches and a few antique apple orchards join vineyards and acres of olive trees, preserving Mendocino's agricultural heritage along the roadsides.

About fifteen miles north of Cloverdale, you enter the Yorkville Highlands American Viticultural Appellation, known for its large ranchland, forests, and small family-owned wineries, of which three are open to the public and the rest by appointment. The surrounding ridges are home to old vine Zinfandel, and intense Pinot Noir, Syrah, and Cabernet Sauvignon.

Another thirteen miles northward and you arrive in Boonville, where art and craft galleries, and restaurants are draws. In the 1850s, residents of the valley developed their own language, known as Boontling. Although there are few fluent speakers of Boontling, remnants of the language are immortalized by signs on pay telephone booths that say *Bucky Walter* (named for the owner of the first telephone in the valley) and restaurants that advertise *bahl gorms*, "good food." Local wine labels tout more Boontling such as Handley Cellars *Brightlighter* (city slicker), Navarro's *Deep End Red* (reference to Navarro at the west end of the valley), and Drew's *Fog Eater* (coast dweller). The Anderson Valley Brewing Company has its own line of Boontling-inspired labels and tours of the brewery.

Bahl gorms are found at the Boonville Hotel and Lauren's Café in Boonville and Libby's in Philo, as well as Gowan's Farm Stand. Markets and other eateries offer a range of fare, such as hamburgers, espresso drinks, ice cream, biscotti, organic meatloaf, Mediterranean cuisine, and Mexican dishes. Many of the wineries have picnic areas.

Or you can pick up some wine at one of the tasting rooms, stop by the Apple Farm, then head to Hendy Woods State Park to picnic under an outstanding grove of old growth redwoods. Another option, when driving through the forested part of Highway 128, is to stop at Dimmick State Park, or wait until you reach the mouth of the Navarro River, stop by Navarro-by-the-Sea education center, and wiggle your toes in the sand on the beach.

YORKVILLE

Halcon Vineyards
www.halconvineyards.com

Judson Hale Winery
www.Jhwinery.com
(707) 433–8488

Le Vin Winery & Vineyards
www.levinvineyards.com
(707) 894–2304

Lone Oak Estate Winery
www.loneoakestatewinery.com
(707) 894–9260

Maple Creek Winery/
Artevino Wines
www.maplecreekwine.com
(707) 895–3001

Marietta Cellars
www.mariettacellars.com
(707) 433–2747

Meyer Family Cellars
www.mfcellars.com
(707) 895–2341

Route 128 Winery
www.route128winery.com
(707) 696–0004

Wattle Creek Winery
www.wattlecreek.com
(707) 894–5166

Yorkville Cellars
www.yorkvillecellars.com
(707) 894–9177

ANDERSON VALLEY

Balo Vineyards
www.balovineyards.com
(707) 877–3727

Baxter Winery
www.baxterwinery.com
(707) 963–0121
Tasting available at The Wine
Bar[n] at Glendeven Inn

Berridge Wine
www.berridgewines.com
(707) 895–9010

Bink Wines
www.binkwines.com
(707) 746–1304

Black Kite Cellars
www.blackkitecellars.com
(415) 923–0277
Tasting available at Sip!
Mendocino

Breggo Cellars
www.breggo.com
(707) 895–9589

Brutocao Cellars
www.brutocaocellars.com
(707) 895–2152

Champ de Réves Vineyards
www.champderevesvineyards.com
(707) 321–6756

Claudia Springs Winery
www.claudiasprings.com
(707) 895–3993

Copain Wines
www.copainwines.com
(707) 836–8822

Couloir Wines
www.couloirwines.com
(707) 968–0919

Demuth Winery
www.demuthwinery.com
(707) 895–3729

Drew Family Cellars
www.drewwines.com
(707) 895–9599

Edmeades Winery
www.edmeades.com
(707) 525–6504

Elke Vineyards
www.elkevineyards.com
(707) 225–7220

Esterlina Vineyards & Winery
www.esterlinavineyards.com
(707) 895–2920

Expression Vineyards
www.expressionwine.com
(707) 226–8569

Foursight Wines
www.foursightwines.com
(707) 895–2889

Frati Horn Wines
www.fratihorn.com
(707) 484–2649

Fulcrom Wines
www.fulcrumwines.com
(732) 610–9602

Goldeneye Winery
www.goldeneyewinery.com
(707) 895–3202

Greenwood Ridge Vineyards
www.greenwoodridge.com
(707) 895–2002

Gryphon Wines
www.gryphonwines.com
(831) 626–2890

Handley Cellars
www.handleycellars.com
(800) 733–3151;
(707) 895–3993

Harmonique-Conzelman
www.harmoniquewine.com
(800) 937–1889

**Tasting with Claudia Springs
in Floodgate Ici/La Bas**
(415) 751–6306

Husch Vineyards
www.huschvineyards.com
(707) 895–3216

Knez Winery Cerise/
Demuth Vineyards
www.knezwinery.com
(707) 895–3494

Lazy Creek Vineyards
www.lazycreekvineyards.com
(707) 895–3623

Littorai Wines
www.littorai.com
(707) 823–9586

Londer Vineyards (Rivers Edge)
www.londervineyards.com
(707) 895–9001

Lula Cellars
www.lulacellars.com
(707) 895–3737

MacPhail Family Wines
www.macphailwines.com
(707) 433–4780

Navarro Vineyards
www.navarrowine.com
(707) 895–3686

Phillips Hill Estates
www.phillipshillestates.com
(707) 895–2209

Philo Ridge Vineyards
www.philoridge.com
(707) 895–3036

Roederer Estate
www.roederer-estate.com
(707) 895–2288

Roessler Cellars
www.roesslercellars.com
(707) 933–4440

Scharffenberger Cellars
www.scharffenbergercellars.com
(707) 895–2957

Standish Wine Company
www.standishwinecompany.com
(707) 895–9213

Toulouse Vineyards
www.toulousevineyards.com
(707) 895–2828

Waits-Mast Family Cellars
www.waitsmast.com
(415) 405–6686

Zina Hyde Cunningham
www.zinawinery.com
(707) 895–9462

U.S. Highway 101-
The Redwood Highway:

Upper Russian River Valleys

From the headwaters of the Russian River above Redwood Valley, and throughout the Ukiah Valley, the Pomo, local Native Americans, established villages long before the Yokayo and Sanel Valley Ranchos became the northernmost Mexican land grants in coastal California. Yokayo is derived from a Pomo word for "deep valley." Bordered by the Mayacamas Mountains on the east, and the Coastal Range to the west, peaks and ridges reach as high as 6,000 feet.

The Redwood Highway has its own history as the route that heads north from the Golden Gate Bridge to the giant redwood (*Sequoia sempervirens*) forests in northern California. It traverses Mendocino wine country from Hopland to Willits, home of the Mendocino County Museum, and continues on past hidden vineyards in the north county.

Fine restaurants abound throughout the Highway 101 corridor in Hopland, Ukiah, Talmage and Redwood Valley, and as you venture further north to Willits and Laytonville, on the way to the tall redwood strees.

Named for the hops grown to make beer, Hopland is the place to slow down and discover the many winery tasting rooms specializing in varietals with roots in Italy, Burgundy, the Rhône or Bordeaux. Passports, in their respective seasons, spur weekends of activities at the wineries, which in addition to being clustered along Highway 101, are located on side roads, including Terra Sávia on Mountain House Road, and Campovida just east on Highway 175. Dining at Piazza de Campovida is a wood-fired pizza extravaganza and the Blue Bird Café is the locals' fave.

Along Highway 101, you'll find wineries with verandas, in a Mediterranean villa, with a redwood grove, with a hillside cave, and with Russian River frontage, before coming to Ukiah, Mendocino County's seat of government. Ukiah has a charming tree-lined downtown. Enoteca, a wine bar, joins Patrona with contemporary local cuisine and an exemplary wine list. Schat's Bakery and North State Café, the locals' meeting places, Oco Time with high end Japanese-style cuisine, and Saucy with wood-fired pizza, represent a few of the inviting downtown restaurants.

Your beer thirst can be quenched at two breweries in Ukiah, the Mendocino Brewing Company and the Ukiah Brewing Company, home to the country's first organic brewpub. The visitor's center, located on Perkins Street, shares the historic train depot with an art gallery, one of many in Ukiah. History buffs and artists will enjoy the Grace Hudson Museum, a gallery saluting Native American Pomo art, as well as special exhibits.

Nearby at the City of Ten Thousand Buddhas, a vegetarian restaurant, Buddhist temple and school are sited among the vineyards on the Talmage bench. To the east, Lake Mendocino is a recreation, bass fishing, camping, and swimming paradise.

Take the Lake Mendocino exit to Parducci Cellars, Mendocino's oldest continuously run winery, where sushi from Oco Time or sandwiches are on hand in the tasting room.

Redwood Valley, at the north end of the key-shaped Ukiah Valley, is the "Little Italy" of Mendocino. A tour around the valley passes the homesteads of Italian descendants of Mendocino's first grape growers. A Taste of Redwood Valley holds a variety of events throughout the year with wine tasting, bounteous food, music and art on the weekend schedules. Many wineries, normally open only by appointment, are open for A Taste of Redwood Valley events.

Potter Valley, reached just past Lake Mendocino on Highway 20, is home of McFadden Farm, and Magruder Ranch, where organic beef and pigs are raised alongside vineyards and hayfields.

Masut is one of the last vineyards in the Ukiah area, at the point where Highway 101 heads uphill past Ridgewood Ranch, home of the famous racehorse Seabiscuit. The Ranch provides tours by reservation at various times throughout the year.

Willits, just to the north, is the home of the Mendocino County Museum and the Roots of Power steam railroad and logging collection, as well as the Skunk Train. At the Museum, you'll find historic artifacts of Mendocino's grape-growing past and the Mendocino Wine History Project, as well as a permanent Seabiscuit exhibit.

A few more vineyards grow north of Willits, including Vin de Tevis on the Eel River near Dos Rios, which is on the way to the Mendocino National Forest. Further north near the town of Laytonville, which also has good restaurants, is Alder Springs Winery, on a hilltop where Cabernet Sauvignon, Merlot and Cabernet Franc grow.

HOPLAND

Albertina Wine Cellars
www.albertinawinecellars.com
(707) 744–1475

Bells Echo
www.bellsechovineyard.com
(707) 744-1260; (415) 898-9751

Bonterra Vineyards
www.bonterra.com
(707) 462–7814
Tasting available at Sip! Mendocino

Brutocao Cellars
www.brutocaocellars.com
(800) 433–3689; (707) 744–1664

Campovida
www.campovida.com
(707) 400–6300

Cesar Toxqui Cellars
www.toxqui.com
(707) 744–1071

DNA Vineyards
www.dnavineyards.com
(707) 463–0782

Duncan Peak Vineyards
www.duncanpeak.com
(707) 744–1129

Fetzer Vineyards
www.fetzer.com
(707) 744–1250

Golden Vineyards
www.goldenvineyards.com
(707) 485–8885

Graziano Family of Wines
www.grazianofamilyofwines.com
(707) 744–VINO (8466)

Jaxon Keys Winery & Distillery
www.jaxonkeys.com
(707) 462–0666

Jeriko Estate Winery
www.jerikoestate.com
(707) 744–1140

McFadden Farm and Vineyard
www.mcfaddenvineyard.com
(707) 744–8463

McNab Ridge Winery
www.mcnabridge.com
(707) 744–1986

Milano Family Winery
www.milanowinery.com
(707) 744–1396

Naughty Boy Vineyards
www.naughtyboyvineyards.com
(707) 743–2868

Nelson Family Vineyards
www.nelsonfamilyvineyards.com
(707) 462–3755

Parducci Wine Cellars
See Ukiah Valley

Patianna Organic Vineyards
www.patianna.com
(800) 397–6101

Rack and Riddle
www.rackandriddle.com
(707) 744–8100

Rosati Family Wines
www.rosatifamilywines.com
(707) 894–3683

Saracina Vineyards
www.saracina.com
(707) 744–1671

Sip! Mendocino Wine Bar
www.sipmendocino.com
(707) 744–8375

Valentine Vineyards
www.valentinevineyards.com
(415) 453–3732

Terra Sávia Winery
www.terrasavia.com
(707) 744–1114

Topel Winery
www.topelwines.com
(707) 744–1787

Weibel Family Vineyards
www.weibel.com
(707) 744–2200

UKIAH VALLEY

Chiarito Vineyard
www.chiaritovineyard.com
(707) 462–7146

Dunnewood Mendocino
georgephelan@wine.com
(707) 462–2985; (707) 467-4841

Embros Wine Company
www.embroswine.com
(707) 462–5774

Germain-Robin Distillery

www.germain-robin.com

 (707) 462–0314

**Parducci Wine Cellars
(also see Hopland)**

www.parducci.com

(707) 462–WINE (9463)

Paul Dolan Wine

www.pauldolanwine.com

Paul Dolan Vineyards

Pauldolan.pdv@live.com

Mendielle Vertu Wines

www.destinationvalley.com

(415) 740–4937

Pettrone Family Cellars

(707) 468–9150

RIVINO

www.rivino.com

(707) 293–4262

Seebass Vineyards

www.Seebassvineyards.com

(707) 467–WINE (9463)

Simaine Cellars

http://simaine.com

(707) 462–6300

Trinafour Cellars

www.trinafourwine.com

(707) 467–0737

Whaler Vineyards

whalerzin@pacific.net

(707) 462–6355

Yokayo Wine Company

www.yokayowineco.com

(707) 463–3366

Redwood Valley/Calpella

Barra of Mendocino

www.barraofmendocino.com

(707) 485–0322

Chance Creek Vineyards

www.bock-ws.com

(415) 834–9675

Cole Bailey Vineyards

www.colebailey.com

(707) 485–9507

Forenzo Vineyards

www.forenzovineyards.com

(707) 234–7171

Frey Vineyards

www.freywine.com

(707) 485–5177

Girasole Vineyards/see Barra

www.girasolevineyards.com

(707)485–0322

Graziano Family of Wines

See Hopland

Masut Winery

www.masut.com

(707) 485–5466

Nonno Giuseppe

www.giuseppewines.com

(707) 485–8458

Oster Wine Cellars

www.osterwine.com

(707) 485–5257

Silversmith Vineyards

www.silversmithvineyards.com

(707) 485–1196

Solmon Tournour Distillery

(707) 485–5112

Testa Vineyards

http://testaranch.com

(707) 485–7051

WestforkCellars

www.westforkwines.com

(707) 327–6541

Potter Valley

Kimmel Vineyards

www.kimmelvineyards.com

(707) 743-1400

Manoir Girard Cellars
www.mjgirard.com; www.pvport.com
(707) 743–1010; (707) 391–9463

McFadden Vineyards
See Hopland

Naughty Boy Vineyards
www.naughtyboyvineyards.com
(707) 743–2868

Tahto Wines
www.Tahtowines.com
 (707)489–8309

EEL RIVER/DOS RIOS/ NORTH COUNTY

Alder Springs Vineyard
www.alderspringsvineyard.com
(707) 984–8970

Vin De Tevis
www.vindetevis.com
(707) 983–8433

Yeilding Art & Wine
www.y-artandwine.com
(707) 326–9355

Mendocino Coast:
Pacific Coast Highway 1

The Pacific Coast Highway, with one winery and several vineyards within sight of the ocean, is included in Mendocino Roots & Ridges for the spectacular coastline and its restaurants and inns that specialize in serving and stocking Mendocino wine. This route offers tasting opportunities and lifestyle amenities that enhance the discover of Mendocino wine.

Along the unspoiled 129-mile coastline from the Lost Coast in the north, a wild and scenic drive commences through picturesque towns, including Westport, Fort Bragg, Caspar, Mendocino, Little River, Albion, Elk, Manchester, Point Arena, Anchor Bay, and Gualala.

The seafood is fresh. From November through March, mussels are harvested from the rocks at low tide; in December, the crab pots go out; in April, we try our luck abalone diving; and the rest of the time, we acquire our seafood from local sources by going to the docks in Noyo Harbor for albacore and salmon, or to local markets that specialize in the catch of the day.

Attractions are plentiful. The lodging on the Mendocino coast is among the best in the world. Like our wineries, most are family-owned and attention to detail and hospitality is renowned. There are also many styles to choose from including motel units on the beach and bed and breakfast inns. Historic places include the Little River Inn, which also has a nine-hole golf course with views of the ocean, a tennis court and celebrated bar and restaurant. The Mendocino Hotel and the MacCallum House Inn join a dozen or so other B&Bs right in the middle of the village of Mendocino, an art-loving community that is on the National Register of Historic Places.

Fort Bragg, the biggest city on the Mendocino Coast, is home to the Skunk Train, which chugs into the forests for a memorable ride and lunch each day. Throughout the year, the Skunk Train offers special wine and culinary events, including their signature Mendocino County Beer, Wine & Mushroom Festival day-long trip in November. The Mendocino Coast Botanical Gardens are the only public gardens on the ocean and are open daily for a picnic or to just walk and admire. It is where Winesong!, Mendocino's wine auction takes place in September.

From Harvest Market in Fort Bragg, to Harvest at Mendosa's in Mendocino, to the Little River Market, the S & B Market in Manchester, Anchor Bay Store, and Village Market and Wine World in Gualala, local foods, cheeses and wines are available. Festivals abound along the coast. Whale festivals in Mendocino, Fort Bragg, Little River and Gualala take place in the early spring, when the gray whales are migrating north with their young. For beer lovers, Fort Bragg is home to the North Coast Brewing Company, which makes Red Seal Ale, Acme and Thelonious, to name a few. Greenwood Gold Apple juice is produced near Drew Family Cellars.

On Mendocino's south coast, from Elk to Manchester, Point Arena to Anchor Bay and Gualala there are restaurants and lodging reflecting one of the county's mottos "another time, another pace."

Styles range from Victorian Gardens' exclusive setting to the onion-dome-topped St. Orres to Mar Vista cottages. The Point Arena Lighthouse, between Manchester and Point Arena, and the Point Cabrillo Lighthouse, between Fort Bragg and Mendocino, both have historic lodging units right on the headlands.

Every season is a good time to visit the coast. In the winter, watching the dramatic surf and pounding rain is a joy from the warmth of cozy inn rooms and restaurants. The coast inns deck out for the holidays and have a week's worth of candlelight tours in December. January finds the Mendocino Crab, Wine & Beer Festival an inspiration for restaurants, the docks, and inns, with winemaker dinners, crab cruises and the Crab Cake Cookoff in Fort Bragg.

With spring, come green grasses, a profusion of flowers, and the whale migrations. Summer brings festivals, such as the Mendocino Music Fest, with two weeks of world-renowned musical performances in a gigantic tent on the State Park headlands in the village of Mendocino. Autumn brings summer-like weather and intermittent rain to fill our forests with a plethora of wild fungi, the stars of the Mendocino County Beer, Wine & Mushroom Festival activities.

See the chapter on Mendocino Festivals and go to www.visitmendocino.com to find out more about where to eat, where to stay and what is going on.

Mariah Vineyards
www.mariahvineyards.com
(707) 882-2243

Pacific Star Winery
www.pacificstarwinery.com
(707) 964-1155

Shandel's Oppenlander
www.shandels.com
(707) 937-5400

The Wine Bar[n] at Glendeven Inn
www.glendeven.com
(707) 937-0083

INDEX

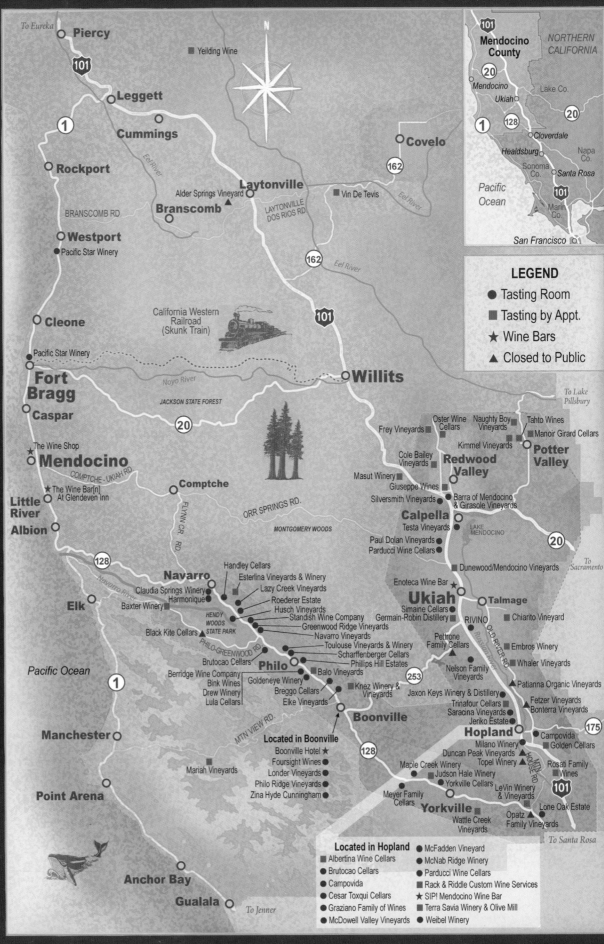